BEAT SELF-DEFEAT

Other Books by John Mason

An Enemy Called Average

Believe You Can—The Power of a Positive Attitude

Be Yourself—Discover the Life You Were Meant to Live

Let Go of Whatever Holds You Back

Never Give Up—You're Stronger Than You Think

Proverbs Prayers

Seize Today

You Can Be Your Best—Starting Today

You Can Do It—Even If Others Say You Can't

You're Born an Original—Don't Die a Copy

The Power of You

BEAT SELF-DEFEAT

Creating a Mindset for ULTIMATE SUCCESS

JOHN MASON

Revell

a division of Baker Publishing Group
Grand Rapids, Michigan

© 2022 by John Mason

Published by Revell
a division of Baker Publishing Group
PO Box 6287, Grand Rapids, MI 49516-6287
www.revellbooks.com

Printed in the United States of America

Library of Congress Cataloging-in-Publication Data
Names: Mason, John, 1955– author.
Title: Beat self-defeat : creating a mindset for ultimate success / John Mason.
Description: Grand Rapids, MI : Revell, a division of Baker Publishing Group, [2022] |
Identifiers: LCCN 2021041400 | ISBN 9780800738914 (paperback) | ISBN 9780800741396 (casebound) |
    ISBN 9781493434336 (ebook)
Subjects: LCSH: Success.
Classification: LCC BJ1611 .M35 2022 | DDC 158.1—dc23
LC record available at https://lccn.loc.gov/2021041400

22 23 24 25 26 27 28   7 6 5 4 3 2 1

I am proud to dedicate this book to my beautiful wife,
Linda; our four great kids, Michelle, Greg, Mike, and
Dave; my mom, Lorene Mason; my two daughters-in-law,
Brittany and Kelley; and my five grandchildren, Emma,
Olivia, Beckett, Darby, and Briggs.

To Linda, for your prayers, laughter, and love.
To Michelle, for your faithfulness and unwavering
    commitment to doing it right.
To Greg, for your deep faith and golf lessons.
To Mike, for your fearless spirit and worshipful heart.
To Dave, for your winning spirit and "Dave and Dad" fun.
To Mom, for your never-ending love and belief in me.
    Dad, I sure miss you!
To Brittany and Kelley, for your love for my sons, my
    grandkids (your children), and the Lord.
To Emma, Olivia, Beckett, Darby, and Briggs, for the
    sweetness, laughter, energy, and abundance of love
    you've brought to our entire family.

Your support, help, encouragement, sense of humor, and
prayers sustain and bless me every day.

Contents

Contents

Introduction

I t's time to get out of our own way and stop being our own worst enemy.

Every person around the world faces this conflict—the battle in our minds. This war is raging around us twenty-four hours a day. It can sometimes seem unrelenting and unfair. That's because the devil is a liar, and our minds can play tricks on us. The good news is, we can remove toxic thinking and replace it with healthy thoughts.

Colossians 3:2 tells us where we should place our minds—on things above. Here's the truth: We get to decide what we think about. We don't have to accept or believe every thought that comes to mind.

Through the encouraging thoughts in this book, I desire to help you discover the power of a godly mindset—acting, thinking, and talking the way God wants you to. If you do, you can find a life of joy, a life of peace with God and your-self, and the opportunity to become all God created you to be—ultimately successful. Proverbs says, "As he thinks in his heart, so is he" (23:7 AMP).

Position yourself to receive all the healthy thoughts God has for you through this book. That's the mindset He desires for you and the one I work on for myself. Be encouraged; God is for you!

Together, let's beat self-defeat!

1 | Me versus Me

Nothing in this world can trouble you as much as your own thoughts. No one has the right to make you feel bad, not even you.

Khalil Gibran said, "My enemy said to me, 'Love your enemy.' And I obeyed him and loved myself." Look in the mirror—that's your competition. Your worst enemy can't harm you as much as your unfiltered thoughts.

I keep my friends close and my enemies closer—that's easy for most of us to do because we're our own worst enemy.

I had finished my day at the office and gotten up from my desk to walk out of the building when I noticed a bump on my knee. This bump was so big, it made my pants stick out on the right side of my kneecap. *I didn't bang my knee on anything!* I thought. *What could it be?* I began to replay my day over and over, convincing myself I had not bumped my knee on anything.

Never build a case against yourself. Don't put water in your own boat; the storm will put enough in on its own. And did you know that the great evangelist Dwight L. Moody said, "I've never met a man who gave me as much trouble as myself"?

I knew I hadn't bumped my knee on anything, and as I thought about it, a second thought came to me . . . *I've had bumps before, but this feels different! It doesn't feel like a bump. It feels like a lump!*

After five minutes of thinking like this, I began picturing myself playing golf with only one leg! You see, through thinking incorrectly, I'd gone from a *bump* to a *lump* to a *stump*! In only five minutes.

By then, I was driving home, and suddenly I realized what I was doing. I said out loud, "John, you're so stupid! I thank You, God, that by Jesus's stripes, I am healed. Your Word says believers can lay their hands on the sick, and they recover!" I laid my hand on my knee, said a prayer, and by the time I got home, that bump was entirely gone. Praise God!

Inaccurate conversations with ourselves give a small thing a big shadow. Those damaging words are the misuse of God's creative imagination placed inside us. The more we listen to our negative thinking, the bigger its shadow grows and darkens what were once bright areas in our lives. Someone once said, "Don't believe the things you think in the middle of the night. You're your own worst enemy, and you can't win that fight."

When wrong thinking comes your way, here's how to win: you can keep "casting down imaginations, and every high thing that is exalted against the knowledge of God, and bringing every thought into captivity to the obedience of Christ" (2 Cor. 10:5 ASV). Instead, I like to tell myself (join with me), "I am who God says I am, I can have what He says

I can have, I can do what He says I can do. I accept how God has made me and choose to say yes to Him."

There's been a lot of talk recently about fake news. There's no more critical fake news than when we tell ourselves we can't do what we know God wants us to do. That news is false, twisted, out of context, and fraudulent. The truth is, as told to Winnie the Pooh by Christopher Robin, "You're braver than you believe, stronger than you seem, and smarter than you think."

Don't believe everything you think. Ralph Marston advised, "There are plenty of difficult obstacles in your path. Don't allow yourself to become one of them."

2 | Fake Diamonds Appear Perfect, but Real Diamonds Have Flaws

What has stolen your joy? Could the thief be perfectionism? Stop letting perfectionism hold you back. It's a dream killer.

Thinking that everything needs to be flawless leads to procrastination and regret. You'll find yourself paralyzed. Imperfections should not be regretted; they're supposed to be learned from and accepted. People are supposed to make mistakes—that's why we have erasers.

I love that the Bible is full of imperfect people, with one notable exception. God did this to encourage all of us very flawed people. You were born to be real, not perfect.

I've had the opportunity to help many authors with their books, and over the course of years, I've come up with several sayings that apply to all my authors. One of my favorite ones is, "There has only been one perfect book, and it's not yours." Authors often believe that what they write has to be perfect. I find this challenge more common with first-time authors. As a result, many times they don't even get the book finished or it's so late that it's lost its opportunity. A flawed diamond is more valuable than a perfect brick.

My hope in saying "there has only been one perfect book, and it's not yours" is to communicate to authors the genuine value of finishing the book as best they can, with what they have, where they are. Then trust God to do what He wants to do through the book. I also recommend that they trust others who are skilled in editing and fine-tuning to help the book become as "perfect" as possible. You don't inspire others by being perfect. You inspire others by how you deal with your imperfections. According to Dejan Stojanovic, "In trying to be perfect, he perfected the art of anonymity, became imperceptible, and arrived nowhere from nowhere."

The Bible says, "If you wait for perfect conditions, you will never get anything done" (Eccles. 11:4 TLB). When God thought of His plans for you, He knew you'd mess up. When you stumbled, He didn't say, "Oh Myself!" Your mistakes are not a surprise to Him. At the end of a long day, don't get into bed, turn off the lights, and then spend eight hours thinking about every mistake you've ever made.

There are three musts that hold us back: I must do it perfectly. You must treat me flawlessly. And the world must be pure.

Pastor Tom (not his real name) was a fantastic worship leader. I had just begun to speak in churches around the country and found myself sitting in the front row as the music started. I could immediately tell he was a talent unlike any other I had seen. He had a natural gift for leading worship. His voice was terrific. It was apparent that he genuinely loved worshiping God. About halfway into the first song, I noticed that he adjusted some dials with his hands and some buttons with his feet while leading the congregation in worship. I'm sure that took a unique talent all of its own, but it also was incredibly distracting. I knew he was a professional and trying to get it "just right." But what was evident to me was that no one could tell the difference based on any change he made, yet it was disrupting his primary goal to help people encounter God through song.

I remember thinking this was a snapshot of life. We become so easily distracted that we get in our own way in the pursuit of perfection.

Pastor Tom came up to me after the service and asked what I thought about the music. I told him it was wonderful but he might want to consider refraining from adjusting the board and the knobs on the foot pedal during the entire worship service. He said he didn't know he was doing that. I guess it had become a habit. Let's stay away from anything that keeps us from doing the main thing.

Here's the excellent news: Pastor Tom had a teachable spirit. What he wanted most was godly worship. He received the correction and enjoyed several wonderful years as the worship leader at that church. Thirty years ago, he founded a church that is still thriving and impactful today.

Here's how *Psychology Today* describes perfectionism:

Perfectionism is a trait that makes life an endless report card on accomplishments or looks. When healthy, it can be self-motivating and drive you to overcome adversity and achieve success. When unhealthy, it can be a fast and enduring track to unhappiness. What makes extreme perfectionism so toxic is that while those in its grip desire success, they are most focused on avoiding failure, resulting in a negative orientation. They don't believe in unconditional love, expecting others' affection and approval to be dependent on a flawless performance.[1]

Don't be like the mom who said, "I didn't know I had a problem with perfectionism until I watched my kids hang ornaments on the tree wherever they wanted." Only God is perfect. He's perfect at perfecting us too. He's God, you're not. The Bible says, "The LORD will perfect *that which* concerns me" (Ps. 138:8, emphasis added). You and I are perfectly imperfect.

God says to come to Him just as you are. Stop being disappointed with everything you *aren't* and start accepting yourself for everything you *are*. I believe it's accurate to blame social media for some of this. It has caused us to display jealous behavior based on illusions. People are envious of things, relationships, and lifestyles that don't even exist. The fastest way to kill something special is to compare it to something else.

Relax. Karen Salmansohn said, "You don't need a perfect life to be happy. You just need to surround yourself with people who love you for who you are." Know that you can stumble, miss the mark, start late, make a wrong decision, look different, be unsure, waver in your faith, start over, and still succeed. Don't worry about being perfect—it will never happen. You can beat the self-defeating thinking of perfectionism.

3 | If God Is Making You Wait, Be Prepared for Great Things

n 1985, Wesley Jones, the principal of Port Barre Elementary School, pulled aside the school's longtime janitor, Joseph "Gabe" Sonnier. He looked at Gabe and said, "I'd rather see you grading papers than picking them up."[1] Jones had remembered Sonnier being a good student at Port Barre and a hard worker.

Sonnier never forgot those words. Even though he continued to be a janitor for fifteen more years, he never ignored the impact that one sentence had on him. So, at thirty-nine years old, while continuing to work full time as a janitor, he decided to shoot for the stars—he started his journey to become a teacher.

"I would come to work at like five in the morning and leave at seven and go to school all day, and then come back and finish up my eight hours of work here, then go home and do homework," he shared with a local television station.[2]

The effort was eventually worth it. Sonnier received his bachelor's degree and became a teacher in one of the very classrooms he used to clean. But Sonnier wasn't finished. He decided to continue his education and get his master's degree. Then his life became even more impressive. In November 2013, Port Barre Elementary School announced its new principal, Joseph Gabe Sonnier. He went from a mop to a master's, thanks to an encouraging word and a persistent spirit.

Someday in your future, people will express profound gratitude to you because you didn't give up today. Your breakthrough is never just about you; it's about all the people who will be blessed and encouraged because you didn't quit.

Winston Churchill said, "Never give up on something you can't go a day without thinking about." It's been said that sometimes life doesn't give you something you want—not because you don't deserve it but because you deserve more.

Don't stop faster than you start. Clint Brown noted, "The world will always give you the opportunity to quit, but only the world would call quitting an opportunity."

Keep the faith. The most amazing things in life tend to happen right at the moment you're about to give up hope. Morgan Harper Nichols writes, "Perhaps you were made for this moment to walk through blazing fire and come forth as gold."

Don't be disappointed with the results you didn't get from the work you didn't do. Galatians 6:9 promises, "Let us not become weary in doing good, for at the proper time we will reap a harvest if we do not give up" (NIV). According to Harvey MacKay, "If you are persistent, you will get it. If you are consistent, you will keep it."

As an author, I have the privilege of signing many books. I like to write encouraging expressions in each book before

I sign my name. One of the most common sayings I write is this: *Never give up!* This simple statement is one of the most powerful success principles ever preached!

People don't fail; they just give up too easily. You'll know you're on the right path when everything stops being easy. No, it won't be easy. Yes, it will change your life when you don't give up.

Two men were shipwrecked on an island. The minute they reached the island, one of them started screaming and yelling, "We're going to die! We're going to die! There's no food! No water! We're going to die!"

The second man was propped up against a palm tree and acting so calm, it drove the first man crazy.

"Don't you understand? We're going to die!"

The second man replied, "You don't understand. I make $100,000 a week."

The first man looked at him quite dumbfounded and asked, "What difference does that make? We're on an island with no food and no water! We're going to *die!*"

The second man answered, "You just don't get it. I make $100,000 a week, and I tithe 10 percent on that $100,000 a week. My pastor will find me!"

When you are persistent, like he knows his pastor is, you know it—and so does everyone else.

Never give up on what you know you should do. Failure is waiting on the path of least persistence. Doing nothing is hard because you never know when you're finished or when you've reached your goal. Persistence can accomplish what talent never will. The "overnight success" spent many days and nights getting there.

4 | "Trust Me," God Whispers

Linda and I were struggling financially like any young married couple who had a child or two. I needed a better job with better pay. We began to agree, in prayer, specifically for an opportunity for me to fully use my talents and gifts.

Within a week or two, I received a phone call out of the blue about an opportunity to be a church administrator at a rapidly growing church in Southern California. Incredibly, the salary was excellent and the job description was what we had prayed for. It was all I desired, plus I would have the freedom to continue to consult. It seemed, at the time, to be the precise answer to prayer that we'd petitioned God for.

I remember my first conversation with the senior pastor about the job. He told me I had come highly recommended from another church that was a consulting client of mine. He was excited for me to fly out to California to interview for the position and to bring Linda and our children along.

Within a matter of weeks, we arrived in California. The day after we arrived, we went to Disneyland with the pastor and his wife. Candidly, they rolled out the red carpet for me, and it seemed like everything was perfect. Except Linda and I both felt something wasn't quite right. But how could that be? This appeared to be the perfect answer to prayer. The job was exactly what we had asked for—and more!

After I returned to Tulsa a week later, the pastor called me and excitedly offered me the job. That unsettled feeling inside me was still there, so I told him I needed to think about it. He seemed quite surprised and slightly irritated by my response. I said I would get back to him within a day or two.

The opportunity at the church was good. It was the most rapidly growing church in his denomination, and he was a tremendous speaker. They had multiple services and standing-room-only crowds. It was a beautiful part of the country; everything looked *right*. But it was *wrong*.

I called the pastor back and told him I was going to decline the offer. I was a little taken aback by his angry retort. He said I was missing God's will and it was *right* for me to take this job. He pressed and asked if I would reconsider. I sincerely told him I would give it more consideration and get back to him.

Over the next couple of days, I talked with Linda and prayed about this opportunity that looked perfect on the surface. But the more we talked and prayed, the more we were sure the opportunity wasn't right for us. *Even though it was exactly what we had prayed for.*

I called the pastor back and told him I was not taking the job and my decision was final. He flatly told me I was missing God's will and making a mistake. Then he hung up.

That's it, I thought.

Three months later, I decided to give him a call, just to see how he was doing. I called the church early in the morning. The receptionist answered. I asked for the pastor, and she told me he was no longer there.

Silence.

I asked, "Well, where is he?" She told me that he had left and wouldn't be returning.

I found out later he'd been having an affair with *two women* in the church (both in the choir) *at the same time.* The church was falling apart.

I guess God knew. No, I *know* God knew. He protected us. I'm glad we didn't move our whole family to California to get right into the middle of that situation. Even though the opportunity looked so perfect, my unknown future was in the hands of the all-knowing God.

Proverbs 16:25 says,

> There is a way that seems right to a man,
> but its end is the way to death. (ESV)

Without a doubt, one of the most powerful opportunities for agreement can occur between a husband and wife. I am thankful Linda and I both found ourselves on the same page regarding this church position. It allowed us to stand together against a wrong decision—a decision that was not just about a job but a bad situation overall.

I've always tried to seek God's peace. And this situation was no exception. Neither one of us could find peace about accepting this offer. We knew the safest place in all the world is in the middle of the will of God.

No matter how things look right now, know that God is still in control of your life. Stay in peace and obey Him. Believe He will always guide you in the right direction.

I heard someone once say, "When I'm worried, it's because I'm trying to do everything myself. When I'm at peace, it's usually because I remember that God is in control." When I put my cares in God's hands, He puts His peace in my heart.

The Bible says to let the peace of God rule in our hearts (see Col. 3:15). The Amplified Bible tells us to let the peace that comes from Christ act as an umpire in our hearts. God's peace can guide us to say "safe" to an idea or "out" to a relationship. Be led by peace. It's always better to miss a few things you should have done than to get into all kinds of things you shouldn't.

When you really think about it, it all comes down to trust. What are you trusting in? Education? Experience? Finances? Ingenuity? Trusting only in any of those things will let you down. Instead, here's the answer from Isaiah 26:3–4:

> You keep him in perfect peace
>   whose mind is stayed on you,
>   because he trusts in you.
> Trust in the LORD forever,
>   for the LORD GOD is an everlasting rock. (ESV)

A real relationship with God has trust.

When God closed the door in California, I knew it was His signal for us to move forward together to the next opportunity He had for us. "Blessed is he who trusts in the LORD" (Prov. 16:20 ESV).

Although we were in the same financial and work situation in the short run, things began to change for the better. Saying *no* freed us to say *yes* to God and some fantastic opportunities right around the corner. Not long afterward, I wrote my first book and began to speak across the country and internationally.

Jesus said, "My peace I give to you" (John 14:27). You'll find great peace and rest in the presence of God. Trouble, nervousness, anxiety, unrest—all these flee in the Lord's presence.

Invite God's presence everywhere you are. James 4:8 promises, "Draw near to God, and he will draw near to you" (ESV). He will encamp around you every minute and be with you in every situation of life. In His presence, you will find great joy and light, divine protection, peace, and rest. The Bible never once says, "Figure it out." But over and over, it says, "Trust God." He's got it all figured out.

In Philippians 4:6–7, the apostle Paul counsels us, "Do not be anxious about anything, but in every situation, by prayer and petition, with thanksgiving, present your requests to God. And the peace of God, which transcends all understanding, will guard your hearts and your minds in Christ Jesus" (NIV).

It isn't the absence of problems that gives us peace; it's God who is with us in the problems. Trust Him today.

5 | Dear Stress, Let's Break Up

A man I met one time owned an organization that later would buy hundreds of thousands of copies of my books and asked me to speak at one of their largest events. Not only would there be more than thirteen thousand people at the Georgia World Congress Center in Atlanta, Georgia, but the audience would consist of only leaders. I love speaking to leaders because I know I'm speaking to the people connected to each leader. It's always an honor to be an influence on influencers.

I was told I would be one of two main speakers that weekend, with the other being Mary Lou Retton, the famous 1984 Olympic gold medal gymnast. Of course, I was excited about the invitation, but as I readied myself to speak, I quickly discovered what the "opportunity" really looked like. From behind the stage, I looked out over the audience. People stretched as far as the eye could see. The atmosphere was electric. People were engaged and excited. Their expectations were something I had never experienced before, and here I was, about fifteen minutes away from giving a forty-five-minute talk to that enormous crowd. Then it hit me. My mouth went completely dry. I mean, dry as the Sahara Desert. Yes, I had what is called cotton mouth. If you know anything about cotton mouth, you understand that you can hardly talk, let alone speak to more than ten thousand people. Since I'd never encountered this before, I started to drink as much water as possible, but I didn't want to drink too much because that could create other, even more embarrassing, problems.

I was anxious. I was stressed. Now only minutes away from speaking to a hungry-to-learn crowd, it came to me what I should do. I realized I had been focusing on myself, not on the people. I needed to change my thinking and pick the proper thought about my situation to replace the troubling thoughts I was having. I recall saying a prayer that went like this: "Lord, I am the lowest person in this room. I am a servant. Help me to bless and encourage these people. Use me for Your glory and help me be able to feel my tongue in my mouth again! Amen!"

By asking for God's help and not focusing on myself, I was now in the correct position to help others—and at the same time help myself. Right before I was introduced to the crowd, as I was climbing the steps backstage, I noticed I could feel my tongue again and my mouth was normal. A supernatural rain had fallen on the desert in my mouth. I was ready to go.

I'll never forget walking onto the stage and being introduced as the theme song from *Rocky* played. My stress was gone; I'd switched my focus. I felt like the lady who said,

"It's astounding how much one's stress level goes down with the simple act of switching from skinny jeans to pajamas." I was comfortable and free to be a servant. Proverbs 12:25 tells us that

> anxiety in a man's heart weighs him down,
> but a good word makes him glad. (ESV)

Anxiety disorders are pervasive. According to the National Institute of Mental Health, an estimated one-third of US adults experience an anxiety disorder at some point in their lives.[1] Millions of people deal with this challenge every single day. Anxiety stops your life; I've seen people I love struggle with how difficult this is. But nothing is too big for God. Nothing.

It's been said that anxiety is like a toddler. It never stops talking and moving around in your personal space. It tells you you're wrong about everything and wakes you up at 3:00 a.m.

My go-to Scripture when I feel the heat of stress is 1 Peter 5:7, "Casting all your care upon Him, for He cares for you." I picture casting what's troubling me to God like I cast a fishing lure to the deepest part of the water. I throw it so far away from me that I can't reach out and get it back. Imagine, right now, that the God of the universe cares about your worries. He is waiting in heaven, ready to receive anything you're troubled by. He desires to take it away and carry it for you.

I'm sure I have asked God hundreds, maybe thousands, of times to take my cares. Doing this keeps me from caring too much about everything and allows His peace to take its place. I know those worrisome thoughts are lying to me. I know I am loved, and it's going to be all right. Let it go, just like the famous song, or you'll be frozen—just like the movie with the same title. You have to surrender and release it, then have faith in what is coming from your heavenly Father. It's in His hands now. For me, nothing diminishes anxiety faster than taking action like this. Storms don't last forever. Spoiler alert: everything is going to be okay.

Never believe the things you tell yourself when you feel sad and alone. The words you say to yourself matter. That loud and lying voice knows your insecurities and tries to use them against you. It doesn't play fair. But God provides a way out. Philippians 4:6–7 says, "Do not be anxious about anything, but in everything by prayer and supplication with thanksgiving let your requests be made known to God. And the peace of God, which surpasses all understanding, will guard your hearts and your minds in Christ Jesus" (ESV).

The devil wants you to think there's nothing more permanent than your temporary situation. No amount of regret can change the past, and no amount of anxiety can predict the future. So instead of criticizing yourself every day, which makes things worse, try accepting who you are in Christ and see how that works. Flip the script—trade a negative thought for the many positive ones found in His Word.

I've heard it said, "God is not in a hurry. You are. It's why you are anxious, stressed, and disappointed." Give your cares to Him right now because He cares so much for you.

6 | Don't Believe Everything You Think

For those of us who were alive, September 11, 2001, is a day we will always remember. Most of us can say exactly where we were when we heard about the Twin Towers falling.

I was scheduled to speak in Buffalo, New York, about two weeks after September 11. I distinctly recall my first flight after that attack—you may be able to as well. Anyone who flew during that time remembers how different the airport experience was.

I was flying from Tulsa to Chicago, then connecting to another flight on my way to Buffalo. Armed officers carrying machine guns were everywhere at O'Hare International Airport in Chicago. Security was quadrupled. Passengers were much more tense than usual. Fortunately, my flight from Tulsa to Chicago was uneventful.

I had decided to preach on fear that Sunday morning, and I was mulling over some of the points I wanted to make.

Little did I know I was about to obtain some more material as I boarded my flight from Chicago to Buffalo.

Because I had been traveling a lot at that time, I received a complimentary upgrade to first class. I remember sitting in my aisle seat as passengers boarded the plane. The atmosphere in the aircraft was very different than before 9/11; people were quiet and nervous.

Nearly all the passengers had boarded the plane when a single man of Middle Eastern descent in his twenties got on carrying a duffel bag. Immediately people began to mumble, "Who is this person? Why is he on this flight?" After a couple more passengers boarded, three other Arab men with backpacks, in their twenties, followed them onboard.

Conversations were now going on among all the passengers in first class, and someone even said out loud, "Let's get those people off this plane." Then a German shepherd–sounding dog began to bark very loudly in the baggage area under the plane. *Is something loaded onto this plane that shouldn't be here?* I wondered as I exchanged glances with my fellow passengers.

I began to feel the fear that I was planning to preach about the following day. The atmosphere was intense. Then four officials from American Airlines boarded the plane and met with the pilot. They weren't gate agents; they were administrative types and were having what looked like a serious conversation. My mind was racing. I was thinking of my family back home and wondering if this was my last day on earth.

After spending about ten minutes in the cockpit, the four officials left the plane and the flight attendant shut and locked the door. The dogs stopped barking. We taxied out and took off. To make matters worse, it was nighttime. I was wondering, *How long before the bomb goes off?* At that point, I'd completely forgotten that I was preaching about fear and worry in about twelve hours.

Of course, as you know, since you're reading this book, we landed safely in Buffalo. No crash, no explosion, only fear robbing me of my peace. Fear is a skilled thief. During that Sunday morning service, I confessed I was now even more an authority on fear and shared my experience on the plane. I'm sure my conviction was stronger than ever.

Fear is the misuse of God's creative imagination that He put inside each one of us. Think about how creative we can be with our fears. Like when we're home alone and every noise we hear is a serial killer. Or how a hangnail can go from an annoyance to a full-blown amputation in a matter of minutes if we let worry take over our imagination.

Fear tricks us into living stagnant lives. Don't let it paralyze you. Remember the saying, "Never be afraid to try something new. Remember, amateurs built the ark; professionals built the Titanic."

Don't be so afraid of being judged that you look for every opportunity to procrastinate. The fears you don't face become your limits. Don't let your fear of what could happen make nothing happen. I agree with D. L. Moody, who said, "Our greatest fear should not be of failure, but of succeeding at something that doesn't really matter."

Worry kills more dreams than failure ever will. Don't let it decide your future. Whatever your desire is, you must want it more than you're afraid of it. Robert Tew noted, "Sometimes what you're most afraid of doing is the very thing that will set you free."

The famous saying is true: *Everything* you want is on the other side of your fears. Set goals that scare you and excite you at the same time. Inhale courage. Exhale fear. Les Brown said, "Too many of us are not living our dreams because we are living our fears."

Hope and fear can't occupy the same space at the same time. That's why we should follow this Scripture: "Casting down imaginations, and every high thing that exalteth itself against the knowledge of God, and bringing into captivity every thought to the obedience of Christ" (2 Cor. 10:5 AKJV). Fear is like fog. When the sun (Son) shows up, it goes away. "I trust in God, so why should I be afraid?" (Ps. 56:4 NLT). Pray as much as you worry, and you'll have less to worry about.

Like Billy in the story I'm about to share, you have two choices concerning your future: fear or faith. A pastor asked little Billy if he said his prayers every night.

"Yes, sir," the boy replied.

"And do you always say them in the morning too?" the pastor asked.

"No, sir," Billy replied. "I'm not scared in the daytime."

Each of us has a choice—we can be positive or negative. Faith filled or fear filled. The phrase "Do not be afraid" is written in the Bible 365 times. That's a daily reminder from God to live fearlessly.

God wants us to walk every day in the same closeness, strength, joy, and direction we experience with Him on Sunday. We don't have to leave that atmosphere of worship and devotion behind just because we leave the building. God is with us . . . period. Every day. The devil wants to ambush us by bringing to our minds fear, doubt, unbelief, and destruction, but fear and worry are interest paid in advance on something we may never own.

Fear is a poor chisel for carving out tomorrow. If you're worried about tomorrow, I have good news for you: Worry isn't reality! Worry is the triumph of fear over faith.

There is a story about a woman who cried profusely while standing on a street corner. A man came up to her and asked why she was weeping. The lady shook her head and replied, "I was just thinking that maybe someday I would get married. We would later have a beautiful baby girl. Then one day, this child and I would go for a walk along this street, and my darling daughter would run into the street, get hit by a car, and die."

It sounds like a pretty ridiculous situation—weeping because of something that will probably never happen. Yet we act this way when we worry. We blow a situation out of proportion that might never come to pass.

The word *worry* is derived from an Anglo-Saxon term meaning "to strangle" or "to choke off." There is no question that worries and fear choke off the positive creativity God gives us.

When fear rises in our minds, we should expect the opposite in our lives. We should expect faith to grow in our hearts to shield us against worrisome thoughts.

Things are seldom as they seem. Haven't we all been frustrated by raisin oatmeal cookies masquerading as chocolate chip?

As we dwell on matters beyond our control, an adverse effect sets in. Too much analysis always leads to paralysis. We must not overthink. We will create a problem that isn't even there.

The Bible says,

> Cast your burden on the LORD,
> And He shall sustain you;
> He shall never permit the righteous to be moved.
> (Ps. 55:22)

Never respond out of fear, and never fear to respond. Action attacks fear; inaction reinforces it.

Don't worry and don't fear. Instead, take your fear and worry to the Lord, "Casting all your care upon Him, for He cares for you" (1 Pet. 5:7). Worry is a route that leads from somewhere to nowhere. Never let it direct your life.

7 | God Is Everywhere and Anywhere You Are

When I work with authors, I always tell them, "When you publish, anything can happen." *Anything* has happened to me many times.

I was invited to speak in Austria at a publishers' conference held in a hotel halfway up a mountain. I remember thinking how beautiful the view was and how treacherous it must be in the winter.

Speaking at this publishing conference was an honor because it was the first of its type in Europe. Now that the walls of Communism were coming down, those who once published Christian writings in secret were operating out in the open. They wanted to learn all they could from American publishers.

A Christian conference was going on at the same time in the hotel. I didn't know the person hosting the meetings, but I thought, *How wonderful! A publishing and an evangelical conference smack-dab in the middle of Austria. Hitler is undoubtedly turning over in his grave!*

I was walking down a hallway to enter the publishing event when I passed a man going in the opposite direction. After we passed each other, I heard a voice behind me ask, "Are you John Mason?" How odd! Who in the world (literally) would know me there?

I turned and said, "Yes, I'm John Mason." The man said he was attending the Christian conference, but he had something to show me.

"Follow me to my room!" he exclaimed. He was excited, and I had no clue why. I followed him to his room, where he showed me a printout of my entire book *An Enemy Called Average* in Bulgarian.

He had translated it from English to Bulgarian and printed it out to take with him on this trip. Then he opened a folder, and in it was a newspaper article. It was an editorial review of my book, picture and all, in Bulgaria's leading newspaper!

He was so proud. I was shocked. How did he know who I was? How had he translated it? Did he know that what he did was technically illegal? I really didn't care. I was excited my book was reaching areas it hadn't been able to go before. I appreciated him and his efforts. I never got a copy of that book, though.

God can find you wherever, whenever.

> When I wake up,
>   you are still with me. (Ps. 139:18 NLT)

He certainly was there directing the man in the hallway that morning in Austria.

Stop every day and look at the size of God. The Bible tells us that the eyes of the Lord are roaming throughout the whole earth so that He can show Himself strong on behalf of people whose hearts are completely His (see 2 Chron. 16:9).

The Lord finds us where we are and, with our obedience, takes us where we ought to go. Charles Spurgeon observed, "Nearness to God brings likeness to God. The more you see God, the more of God will be seen in you." God is not distant. "The LORD is near to all who call upon Him" (Ps. 145:18).

You are as close to God as you choose to be. So every day, do something that will lead you closer to Him. Don't let the noise of the world keep you from hearing the voice of the Lord.

God shows He's near in every book of the Bible. Realize God has you in His sight and in His hands. He's there when you draw near to Him, and He shows up when you praise Him. He's never more than a prayer or a praise away. He's right there when you're at your best and when you're at your worst. Reach out to Him today.

Nothing—not even bad things or tall mountains and meetings halfway around the world—can separate you from God and His relentless love for you (see Rom. 8:38–39).

8 | God Is at Work When You Least Expect It

Let's frame our minds knowing God is the Alpha and the Omega, the beginning and the end—and everywhere in between. Don't fear the future; God is already there. And He's working on our behalf. A key to thinking accurately is knowing God knows our future. Sometimes when it seems like He's the least involved in our life, He's actually the most involved.

I find it helpful to look backward and see how God was there all the time—orchestrating, arranging, leading, and directing. Knowing He was there helps my mind have peace about my future. Joshua 1:9 says, "Have I not commanded you? Be strong and courageous. Do not be afraid; do not be discouraged, for the LORD your God will be with you wherever you go" (NIV).

It all really comes down to trust. Proverbs 3:5–6 says, in effect, to trust in the Lord with all our hearts and do not depend on our own understanding; everywhere we go, acknowledge Him and He will direct our paths.

I was starting my first week at college and had enrolled in freshman English, like all the rest of my classmates. It was an early morning class, so each student was slowly trying to find a seat.

I spotted a cute brunette and decided to sit next to her. I hadn't yet bought my syllabus for the class. She, however, had happened to obtain two syllabi for the course (who gets two?).

Perfect!

When she discovered I didn't have a syllabus, she happily gave me her extra one. Not long afterward, I asked her out on a date. I've been dating her ever since. That beautiful girl is my wife, Linda. This story is also the perfect reflection of our relationship: she had two syllabi and I had none.

We can meet thousands of people without any of them really affecting us. And then we meet one person, and our lives are changed forever. It's wonderful to know that God is working on our behalf even when we least expect to see it!

As I was writing this, I realized I was thinking of Linda, and I began to wonder how long she'd been on my mind. Then it occurred to me: since I met her. She's never left it.

Imagine a year from now and realize that today God is already working on our behalf. He knows the end from the beginning. And the beginning from the end. Just because something hasn't worked out for us now doesn't mean there's nothing big in store for us in the future.

To quote Dr. Meredith Grey from *Grey's Anatomy*, "We spend our whole lives worrying about the future, planning for the future, trying to predict the future, as if figuring it out will cushion the blow. But the future is always changing." We don't have to know everything today. We just need to trust Him with our future.

The best thing about the past is that it shows us what not to bring into the future. And just because the past didn't turn out like we wanted it to doesn't mean our future can't be better than we ever imagined.

Corrie ten Boom said, "Never be afraid to trust an unknown future to a known God." Don't worry about tomorrow—God is already there working on your behalf. He's for you, not against you.

What a wonderful thought it is that some of your best days haven't happened yet. It's okay to have a "holy hunch" that your heavenly Father is in your future arranging people, places, ideas, provision, protection, and so much more for you.

9 | Never Let People Who Aren't Going Anywhere Take You with Them

More than thirty years ago, the church I was attending hosted a once-a-month men's luncheon at a local restaurant. They served an excellent buffet, and a speaker shared for twenty minutes before we all went back to work. At this point in my life, I could only be described as a very unsuccessful person. If you had told me you wanted to be successful, I would have said to look at my life and do the opposite!

I will never forget one particular luncheon that became a defining moment in my life. I remember eating and listening to the speaker. I don't recall what I ate or what he said, but I do remember what happened next. I found myself lingering at the restaurant, sitting around a table with five or six other men. I can best describe them as "unproductive Christians." You know the kind of people I'm talking about; the ones who have had four jobs the past two years. The people who are always saying, "God told me this, God said that." They're flying off in one direction one month, then in another the next month, and then in the completely opposite direction the next month. All talk, no action.

I was hanging out with them way past lunchtime—until a quarter to two in the afternoon! That should tell you how much work I had to do, how diligently I worked, and how focused my priorities were.

And if you had really listened to our words, guess what you would have found us talking about? We were all talking about *why we weren't successful*. I was participating in the conversation right along with everyone else. In fact, at that time in my life, I was an authority on the subject.

Suddenly, right in the middle of our conversation, I sensed God speaking to my heart. This is what I heard: "John, there are some people I don't want you to be around anymore." And then He gave me their names. He continued, "There are some people you can be around, but only for a limited amount of time in certain circumstances." Again, He gave me their names.

What's great about God is that when He takes you out of darkness, He doesn't leave you in the dusk. He brings you into the light.

He continued to speak to my heart. "There are some people I want you to be around!" And He gave me three names. These were men who knew me. They saw God's gifts in me and His calling for my life. When I was around them, they

45

brought out the best in me. I was even nicer to my wife after I was around them!

I immediately got up from that table. I remember walking to the southwest corner of the restaurant parking lot. I pointed my finger toward heaven and said, "I'll do it!" Then I drove straight home (back then, you had to go there to make phone calls). I picked up the phone, and I called those three men. I said, "I hope you don't mind, but I need to get together with you on a regular basis." They all said yes.

My life changed!

I noticed a change *that day* as I chose to associate with the right people. Since then, I've tried to be best friends with those who bring out the best in me (and me in them).

You are only going to be as good as the people you choose to surround yourself with. Stay away from negative people. They have a problem for every solution. Be brave enough to let go of those who keep weighing you down.

As you read this and if names come to you, I encourage you to act. You may need to say no to someone or invest more time with someone else. Sometimes the answer to your prayers is a change in your relationships.

If you hang around five confident people, you will be the sixth.

If you hang around five smart people, you will be the sixth.

If you hang around five successful people, you will be the sixth.

If you hang around five idiots, you will be the sixth.

My friend Joe Braucht, who pastors a great church called Destiny Christian Church in Minnesota, lists excellent signs of character to watch for in his 5 Qualities of People in Your Inner Circle:

1. They are committed to Jesus and His Church.
2. They are going where you're going.
3. They have a good spirit.
4. They have good character.
5. They want the best for you.

God has the right associations for you. You'll know who they are because they will feed your soul and you'll feel good after spending time with them. Invest your time with those who love you unconditionally. Don't waste it on those who only love you when the conditions are right.

I'm thankful for the people who have walked into my life and made it better. And I'm grateful for the ones who have walked out and made it better. God puts people in your life for a reason and removes them from your life for a better reason.

Your best friends are those who bring out the best in you. I love people I can joke around with and have a lot of fun with and then have a deep conversation with as well, and it doesn't feel weird at all.

I agree with Kim Culbertson, who said, "People think being alone makes you lonely, but I don't think that's true. Being surrounded by the wrong people is the loneliest thing in the world."

The less you associate with some people, the more your life will improve. When you stay away from unproductive, negative people, good things will start happening for you, and it won't be a coincidence.

Make sure everybody in your "boat" is rowing and not drilling holes when you aren't looking. Think about it: Don't many of your sorrows spring out of relationships with the wrong people?

A good friend knows all your stories. A best friend helped you write them. I've heard it said that a true relationship is two imperfect people refusing to give up on each other. Life is meant for good friends and great adventures. The most valuable antique is an old friend.

We need to be careful of the kind of insulation we use in our lives. We need to insulate ourselves from negative people and ideas, but we should never insulate ourselves from godly counsel and wisdom.

Misery wants our company. In Proverbs, we read, "A mirror reflects a man's face, but what he is really like is shown by the kind of friends he chooses" (27:19 TLB). Proverbs also tells us,

> He who walks with wise men will be wise,
> But the companion of fools will be destroyed. (13:20)

We become like those we associate with. I've found it is better to be alone than in the wrong company. A single conversation with the right person can be more valuable than years of study.

When we surround ourselves with the right kind of people, we enter into the God-ordained power of agreement:

> Two can accomplish more than twice as much as one, for the results can be much better. If one falls, the other pulls him up; but if a man falls when he is alone, he's in trouble. . . . And one standing alone can be attacked and defeated, but two can stand back-to-back and conquer; three is even better,

for a triple-braided cord is not easily broken. (Eccles. 4:9–10, 12 TLB)

Stay far away from negative-thinking "experts." You may have to go alone. Not everyone who starts with you finishes with you. Remember: in the eyes of average people, average is always considered outstanding. Look carefully at the closest associations in your life; they indicate the direction you're heading.

10 | Don't Attend Every Distraction You're Invited To

Focus on the positive and be grateful. A successful businessman parked his brand-new Bentley in front of his office, ready to show it off to his colleagues. As he was getting out, a truck came along too closely and completely tore off the door on the driver's side.

Fortunately, a police officer in his patrol car was close enough to see the accident and pulled up behind the Bentley with his lights flashing. Before the officer had a chance to ask any questions, the man started screaming hysterically about how his Bentley, which he had just purchased the day before, was completely ruined and would never be the same, no matter how any auto body shop tried to make it new again.

After the man finally calmed down from his rant, the officer shook his head in disbelief. "I can't believe how materialistic you are," he said. "You're so focused on your possessions that you neglect the most important things in life."

"How can you say such a thing?" asked the man.

The officer replied, "Don't you even realize your left arm is missing? It was severed when the truck hit you!"

"Oh no!" screamed the man. "My Rolex!"

Focus on what's important. The typical golf ball has over four hundred small dimples. Those tiny impressions allow the ball to fly farther and straighter. Many top professional golfers have discovered this effective technique: they focus on one small dimple before they putt or drive the ball. Narrowing their focus leads to straighter putts and longer drives. What is the dimple in your life you need to concentrate on to gain extraordinary results? Laser in on it and watch what happens.

To gain greater focus, I give you permission to ignore some things. Ignore certain people. Overlook the overly urgent request. Snub that person with ulterior motives. Ignore inaccurate statements made about you by others. Don't let the noise of the world keep you from hearing the focused voice of the Lord. Instead, center yourself; this is your time. At any point, you have the power to say, "No, this is not how the story is going to end." Focus on results, not regret. On impact, not approval.

If the devil can distract you from your time alone with God, then he can isolate you from the help that comes from God alone. Leave alone what truly doesn't matter. Warren Buffett said, "Knowing what to leave out is just as important as knowing what to focus on." Life is short. Concentrate on what matters and let go of what doesn't. What you focus on, you give strength and momentum to. What are you giving your attention to today that is taking you closer to where you want to be tomorrow?

Your mission is too important to give in to distractions. Don't let the noise of the world keep you from hearing the voice of the Lord. It's during our darkest moments that we should focus on the light of God's Word. We are so scared of being judged that we look for every excuse to be distracted. If we focus on the parts of our day that we control—we'll be happier. Focus and effort are within our command.

There comes a time in our lives when we must learn to say *no* to many good ideas. The more we grow, the more opportunities we will have to say no. One key to results is becoming honed in. Nothing brings the concentration needed like the word *no*! Perhaps no other key to growth and success is as overlooked as this one. The temptation is always to do a little bit of everything. Instead, be single-minded about the most important things.

Remember, saying no to a good idea doesn't mean saying *never*. No may mean *not right now*.

The word *no* has power. No is an anointed word that can break the yoke of overcommitment and weakness. No can be used to turn a situation from bad to good, from wrong to right. Saying no can free us from burdens we don't need to carry right now. No can also allow us to devote the correct amount of attention and effort to God's priorities in our lives.

Steve Jobs said, "People think focus means saying yes to the thing you've got to focus on. But that's not what it means at all. It means saying no to the hundred other good ideas that there are. You have to pick carefully. I'm actually as proud of many of the things we haven't done as the things we have done. Innovation is saying no to a thousand things." Focus does not mean saying yes; it means saying no. Effectiveness begins with elimination. Eliminate the unnecessary. To achieve success, stop asking for permission from others who may not have your best interest at heart.

You can't accomplish big things if you're distracted by small things. Be about actions, not distractions. You must starve your distractions and feed your focus. There will always be distractions if you allow them. No more distractions; this is the time to be selfish. Maybe you're not accomplishing what you want because you are simply unclear about what you are asking for. You get what you focus on, so focus on what you want. Dr. John DeMartini said, "If you do not fill your day with high-priority actions that inspire you, your day will fill up with low-priority distractions that will not."

It's easy to remember past situations in which *no* or *not right now* would have been the correct answer. Don't put yourself through that kind of stress in the future. Learn the power of no. *Yes* and *no* are the two most important words you will ever say. These two words determine your destiny. How and when you say them will affect your entire future.

Saying no to lesser things means saying yes to priorities in your life.

11 | Sometimes the Smallest Decisions Can Change Your Life Forever

We have no right to complain about what we permit. Some of our troubles continue because we decide to allow them.

I had just begun to travel and speak in churches when I received an invitation from a church in Buffalo, New York. The pastor was a wonderful man who had a church in downtown Buffalo and connections to other churches in the area. He arranged for me to speak in his church and several others while I was there.

I was new to all of this, so I pretty much accepted whatever arrangements people set up for me. On the phone, before I arrived, the pastor told me that one of his essential prerequisites for all traveling ministers was that they stay in his house and fellowship with some of his church members. He picked me up at the airport and drove me straight to his house, where a group of about a dozen church members greeted us. We had a wonderful dinner together and spent several hours talking about how good the Lord had been in each of our lives.

When I'd first arrived, the pastor told me to put my luggage in a bedroom down the hallway from where dinner was being served. I noticed a small bed in the room but didn't think much of it. After the dinner concluded and everybody left, the pastor directed me back to that same room and told me we would have breakfast at the house in the morning and then go over to the church.

The door behind me closed. I stood alone in the room, looking at the smallest bed I had ever seen. I wondered if he was joking with me or trying to pull a prank. The bed was maybe half the size of a twin bed. I laid on it with my feet hanging off the end—and I'm only five feet, eight inches tall. I had absolutely no room to turn right or left without landing on the floor. I was about to sleep at attention all night!

I didn't sleep very well and kept dreaming about falling off a cliff, to my right and then to my left, all night long. I woke up the following day thankful I was alive, ate breakfast, and then preached the best sermon I could.

I decided from that point forward I was only going to sleep in hotels with regular beds and never again in someone's house. I never figured out why he put me in that room with that bed. But I took away these lessons, straight from the Bible: "You do not have because you do not ask," and "Ask and you will receive" (James 4:2 NIV; John 16:24 NIV).

Successful people make decisions based on where they want to be. Decide something today that your future self will thank you for. Being decisive is not easy. Sometimes the most challenging thing and the right thing are the same.

Too many of us lose hope or feel less free simply because we allow it. We all need to be more decisive. No decision is a decision. The road of life is paved with flat squirrels who ran into the middle of the road then couldn't decide which way to go. You're a product not of your circumstances but rather of your decisions. Results and success follow commitment and decisions.

Do you say this? "I used to be indecisive, but now I'm not sure."

Singer Zayn Malik observed, "There comes a day when you realize turning the page is the best feeling in the world because you realize there is so much more to the book than the page you were stuck on." You can't start the next chapter if you're still reading the first one.

Indecision is deadly. Some of the most miserable people are those who can never make a decision. When the mind is in doubt, it is easily swayed by slight impulses, opening the door to many wrong decisions. Many times indecision causes things to go from bad to worse. The middle of the road is a dangerous place to be; you can get hit by traffic going in both directions. How will you know if it's the right decision if you never make it? It's been said that "a man with one watch knows what time it is; a man with two watches is never quite sure."

One day you'll realize you're very glad you didn't settle for just anything. You chose God's plan. The Bible says to let the peace of God rule in our hearts (see Col. 3:15). Always make decisions that are led by peace.

If you are neutral on spiritual matters, eventually you'll find yourself operating against heaven. Thank God we serve a decisive Lord. He has given us His peace and His Word so that we can make wise decisions. We should not be the kind of people who claim that God has told us one thing this week and the very opposite next week. God does not change in such quick degrees, nor does He ever direct anyone to act contrary to the good sense and sound judgment shown in His Word. It's not hard to make decisions when you know what you believe.

We believers should be the most decisive of all people. Leaders should have wills, not wishes. The Bible says, "A double minded man is unstable in all his ways" (James 1:8 KJV). An indecisive person allows instability to creep into every area of their life. If we don't decide what is important to us, we will only do what is important to others. A greater degree of wishful thinking leads to a greater degree of mediocrity. Being decisive, being focused, and committing ourselves to fulfill a dream significantly increases our probability of success while closing the door to wrong options.

Mediocrity is a region bound on the north by compromise, on the south by indecision, on the east by past thinking, and on the west by a lack of vision. Ask yourself, What one decision would I make if I knew it would not fail?

God wants you to be decisive. If the devil controls your will, he controls your destiny. But if God controls your will, then He controls your destiny. Don't linger over bad decisions; it gives them the power to define you. Forgive yourself and replace them with good ones in the future.

The choice is yours. Don't base your decisions on the advice of those who don't have to deal with the results. Be decisive. Don't be a person who says, "My decision is maybe, and that's final."

Consider this from Kelvin Mamidi:

> There are moments in life when you must make some really hard decisions. Decisions that . . . break your heart. Decisions that seem to kill your breaths. Decisions that make it seem like the end of everything. But maybe those are the decisions that are meant to take your life to better places. Places that you never believed were within your reach. Places that you never knew existed. Places that had forever been waiting for you to make that one decision.

The risk of a wrong decision is preferable to the terror of indecision. Be decisive, even if it means you'll sometimes be wrong. Have the courage to be decisive. Courageous decisions make great stories. Make decisions that will benefit generations to come. Your choices affect others.

Don't settle for the "short bed" your whole life. As author Lewis Carroll reflected, "In the end, we only regret the chances we didn't take, the relationships we were afraid to have, and the decisions we waited too long to make."

12 | When You Fall, Pick Something Up

Sometimes I feel I'm an authority on failures and mistakes. I have so much experience.

Years ago, I was invited to speak at a church I had never been to before by a pastor I had never met. I had an early morning flight, so I was up before the break of dawn finishing my packing. I put everything in my suitcase and rushed off to the airport.

After thirty minutes in the air, I began to replay my morning, checking off in my mind everything I had packed. Suit? Check. Shirts? Check. Shoes? Check. Suddenly I wondered, *Did I bring my notes?* Yes. *My Bible?* Wait . . . I'm not sure. I immediately looked inside my carry-on bag. No Bible! It was nowhere to be found, no matter how many times I searched my bag.

I felt slightly panicked. Here I was, flying to a new church led by a pastor I'd never met. I didn't want to walk off the plane, introduce myself, and then say, "Pastor, may I borrow your Bible?" I could only imagine him thinking, *Who have I entrusted my Sunday service to?*

I had to do something about this situation. I came up with what I thought was a good idea: I would get a Bible in the airport. Yes, I would find a bookstore and buy a Bible. But then I thought what you're probably thinking—*I've never seen a Bible for sale in the airport.* I began to get desperate.

I deplaned as fast as possible and made a beeline for the first store I could find that was selling books. "Do you sell Bibles?" I asked hopefully. "No" was the immediate response. I hurried to find another store. Again, I asked for a Bible. Similarly, the answer was no, but the clerk offered me some hope. She said, "I think the bookstore in the other terminal sells Bibles, so you should go there."

By then, I should have been in baggage claim picking up my luggage, but I decided to run over to the other terminal in one last desperate attempt to secure a Bible. Hurriedly, I passed gate after gate until I saw a bookstore. I headed straight for the cashier and, slightly out of breath, asked, "Do you sell Bibles?"

"Yes, we do," she cheerfully replied. "Let me go get one for you." Relieved, I waited. Only a minute later, she appeared and handed me a small, white baptismal-type gift Bible. I thought, *I didn't pack a white suit, white shirt, white tie, and white shoes. I can't preach from this little white Bible!* But I was desperate, so I purchased it.

I quickly left the terminal and went down the escalator toward baggage claim. As the moving steps went downward, I looked to my right and left, hoping to see a "pastor-looking" person. As I got to the bottom of the escalator, I saw a man alone looking all around. I knew I had found him.

I went straight up to him and introduced myself. He said, "Thank goodness it's you! Here's your bag—it was the only one left."

We walked to his car in the underground parking lot and left the airport. Five minutes into our ride, he asked, "Would you like to go to the church before we go to the hotel? I'd like to show you our latest addition." Usually, I'd rather just head to my room. But suddenly I thought, *A church! They'll have Bibles!* I enthusiastically replied, "Yes!"

It wasn't long before we arrived at the church, and I made it a point to follow just a little behind him. We walked into the impressive main lobby, then continued toward the beautiful sanctuary. As we were about to enter, I spotted a box to my left. On it was a Lost and Found sign.

My heart began to beat a little faster; I was hoping my search would soon be over and I could keep my dignity intact. Following the pastor, I walked beside the box and looked inside. There it was, a beautiful Bible! In one smooth motion, I reached in and "found" that Bible.

That whole weekend I preached with "my" new Bible. But in the back of my mind, I wondered if someone out in the congregation was looking at me, thinking, *That guy's got my Bible!*

Before I left the church, I discreetly returned the Bible to the lost and found so whoever lost it could claim it. What a happy find that Bible was!

We all make mistakes. Some are funny, and some affect us for a lifetime. Everyone has struggles and regrets from the past. But we are not our mistakes.

The first step to overcoming mistakes is to admit them. We can't get past their hold without doing this. One of the most remarkable Scripture verses promises us this. "If we confess our sins, He is faithful and just to forgive us our sins and to cleanse us from all unrighteousness" (1 John 1:9). Wow! Thank You, God. Boy, have I needed this Bible verse in my life.

God loves you so very much. He forgives you, cleanses you, *and doesn't stop there.* He additionally gives you a right standing before Him again. There is no way to fully express my gratitude to Him for this! Zig Ziglar advised, "Don't let the mistakes and disappointments of the past control and direct your future." They don't define you. You are free when you give them to God.

In Japan, some broken objects are not automatically thrown away or mended with superglue but amazingly sometimes repaired with gold. Instead of it being deemed a worthless object, the damage is seen as a unique part of the object's story, which adds to its uniqueness. When repaired with gold, it now becomes more valuable than when it was whole. Consider this when you feel broken by a wrong action: God's purpose for you is more significant than your mistakes—or breaks.

Has failure gone to your head? Just because you failed doesn't mean you're a failure. Nelson Mandela said, "I never lose. I either win or I learn." Don't stop after a failure; dust yourself off, learn the lesson, and start again. When you get knocked down, get back up. Remember the call is higher than the fall.

Failure doesn't mean nothing has been accomplished; there is always the opportunity to learn something. God isn't surprised by your stumbles. His love, grace, mercy, and forgiveness are bigger than any mess you make.

We all experience failure and make mistakes. In fact, successful people always have more failures in their lives than average people do. Great people throughout history have all failed at some point in their lives.

Those who don't expect anything are the ones who are never disappointed. Those who never try, never fail. Anyone who is currently achieving anything in life is simultaneously risking failure. It is always better to fail in doing something than to excel at doing nothing. People who have no failures also have few victories.

How do you respond to failure? You will get knocked down; it is how fast you get up that makes all the difference. There is a positive correlation between spiritual maturity and how quickly a person responds to failures and mistakes. Spiritually mature individuals have a more remarkable ability to get up and go on than spiritually immature people. The less mature the person, the longer they hold on to past failures.

God never sees any of us as failures; He only sees us as learners. We fail only when we don't learn from each experience. The decision is up to us—we can choose to turn a failure into a hitching post or into a guidepost in our lives.

Here are the keys to getting free from the stranglehold of past failures and mistakes:

1. Learn the lesson and forget the details.
2. Gain from the experience, but do not roll the minute details of it over and over in your mind.
3. Build on the knowledge and move forward in your life.

Sherman Finesilver said, "Don't worry about failure. Worry about the chances you miss when you don't even try." Someone else's failure in a particular area does not guarantee *your* failure. Most people fail because they are too afraid to even try. They don't begin due to the fear of failure. Thomas Edison, one of the world's greatest inventors, put it best: "I failed my way to success."

13 | Cinderella Is Proof That a New Pair of Shoes Can Change Your Life

Every little girl loves the fairy tale of Cinderella. It's a story of love, dreams, and change. The dramatic transformation in the young princess, Cinderella, happens from the top of her head down to her glass slippers and offers a lesson for all of us. When we embrace change, something magical happens.

When I reached my late forties, I realized I needed to use a bigger font for my sermon notes. I also started to read my Bible while I spoke with my right arm extended farther and farther out to see the words clearly. (Maybe you're nodding your head right now!)

One Sunday morning, I was ministering in a church in Southern California. The service was going well. I was sharing from the Word, with my Bible extended on my outstretched arm. Right in the middle of my sermon, I couldn't help but notice a lady get up from her seat, turn down the center aisle, and walk out of the sanctuary. I thought about it for a second and then continued.

About ten minutes later, I saw that same lady return and walk down the center aisle, but instead of returning to her seat, she walked all the way to the pulpit where I was standing and handed me a box. I stopped my message and opened the box. Inside was a brand-new large-print edition of the version of the Bible I was using. She had just purchased it in the church bookstore!

I've been using that Bible ever since.

Change is necessary. If you don't change, you'll be left behind. Like the printed words in that Bible, your life becomes more unclear when you don't adjust. Sometimes you will discover what you need to change on your own. Other times, people will let you know. They will stop buying, listening, calling, texting, or they'll just go away. No matter where or how the discovery happens, we all need to change to improve and grow. John C. Maxwell said, "Change is inevitable . . . growth is optional."

Many years ago, I became the leader of a publishing company that had not performed very well. It had suffered thirteen consecutive quarterly losses and cost the owner more than one million dollars since he purchased it. (He later told me he was going to shut it down if we were not able to turn it around in one year.) One thing I knew for certain was that changes were needed. Radical changes.

So, my first day, I looked at every area in the company and began to make substantial changes to strategy, marketing, author acquisitions, and personnel. Beginning the very first week, some of the staff came into my office complaining, "That's not the way we do it," "We've never done it that way," "That won't work." But I knew the opposite was true. To turn this company around, we had to *not* do what we had always done. In fact, after only a couple of weeks, I put a large sign behind my desk in my office that read, "If that's the way it's always been done then that means we need to change it!" Amazingly, all the complaints stopped. The changes were made. And we went on to have miraculous, profitable success. Success that never would have occurred without change.

Sadly, too many people associate staying the same with being spiritual. Change is spiritual and painful. Author Mandy Hale noted, "But nothing is as painful as staying stuck somewhere you don't belong." I believe in following your heart but taking your brain with you.

Christians should embrace change better than anyone else. We have the Holy Spirit to guide us! Many great verses should give us comfort when we're facing change. Scripture promises us that God will

- guide us with His eye (see Ps. 32:8),
- direct our steps (see Prov. 16:9), and
- be a light and lamp to our path and our feet (see Ps. 119:105).

It takes courage to let go of the familiar and embrace the new. If others don't embrace your change, just tell them, "I'm currently under construction. Thank you for your patience."

It's revealing how someone who was just a stranger last year can mean so much to you now. It's sad how someone who meant so much to you last year can be a stranger now. It's interesting how things can change in a year. Sometimes you need to say, "I'm making some changes in my life. If you don't hear anything from me, you are one of them."

The sad truth is, most people are afraid of change. But don't be scared to do or be something different, because it's leading you to a new beginning. Change before you have to. You might need to tell people, "You may not recognize this new me; I'm rearranging the pieces."

Many people underestimate their capacity for change. There is never a perfect time to do a challenging thing. Step out and make the change. I agree with Robin Sharma, who said, "All change is hard at first, messy in the middle, and gorgeous at the end." If you don't like where you are, move. You are not a house.

Change is hard because people overestimate the value of what they have and underestimate the value of what they may gain by giving that up. Karen Salmansohn observed, "What if I told you ten years from now your life would be exactly the same? Doubt you'd be happy. So why are you so afraid of change?"

Your life does not get better by chance; it gets better by choice. Sorry is not enough. Sometimes you actually have to change. Sometimes God places you in uncomfortable circumstances; otherwise, you will never move.

If you aren't changing, you're dying. If you change nothing, nothing will change. If you do not change your path, you will end up where you are heading.

Choose real change, not rearrangements like Wendy Liebman made: "My husband wanted one of those big-screen TVs for his birthday. I just moved his chair closer to the one we already have."

When God wants you to grow, He makes you uncomfortable. Imagine if you woke up one day next week and decided you didn't want to feel the way you do anymore or ever again. And you changed!

Rick Godwin said, "One reason people resist change is that they focus on what they have to give up, rather than what they have to gain." Life improves by change. The two are intrinsically connected. If nothing changed, there would be no butterflies.

Paul Coelho writes, "Close some doors today, not because of pride, incapacity, or arrogance, but simply because they lead you nowhere." It's amazing how drastically your life can change when you stop accepting the stuff you hate and embrace change. Unless your name is Google, stop acting like you know everything.

We are custom built for change. Any one of us can change at any point in time, at any age. Changing doesn't always mean doing the opposite. Most of the time, it means adding to or slightly adjusting what already exists.

Here are three things we know about the future: First, it isn't going to be like the past. Second, it isn't going to be exactly the way we think it's going to be. Third, the rate of change will take place faster than we anticipate.

Nothing remains as constant as change. Even the most precious gems need to be chiseled and faceted to achieve their best luster. Don't end up like concrete—all mixed together and permanently set.

In Isaiah, the Lord declares,

Behold, the former things have come to pass,
And new things I declare;
Before they spring forth I tell you of them. (42:9)

I believe one of the main reasons the Bible was written was to teach us in advance how to respond to many of the changes and situations we would encounter in life. When I was coaching basketball many years ago, I told my players they could prepare ahead of time for situations they'd face on the court. We used to practice as many game conditions as possible so they would already know how to respond when they found themselves in the actual situations. This one idea helped our teams to be very successful.

Choose to flow with God's plan. Be sensitive to the new things He is doing. Stay flexible to the Holy Spirit and know that God directs, adjusts, moves, corrects, and changes you.

Change is a statement of hope. If you're choosing to do something different, you are saying you believe in what God has for you tomorrow. And you choose to be part of it.

14 | Image Is Everything?

Man looks at the outward appearance, but the LORD looks at the heart" (1 Sam. 16:7). Don't get duped into thinking your life means less than a seemingly ideal person's life. Everyone has faults.

Instead, know this: You are the most uniquely gifted and equipped person on the face of the earth to do what God has called *you* to do. Out of billions of applicants, you're the most qualified.

Comparison is never proof. Don't always trust what you see. Even salt looks like sugar. Facebook and Instagram are great places to look at pictures of the fake lives of all the people you don't really know. Even those who tell the truth online are only showing you their highlight reel.

It's amazing the clarity and peace of mind that come from not caring about what anyone else is doing and instead focusing all your efforts on being the person God has called *you* to be. All that energy spent on worrying and feeling second best or nothing at all instantly fades away and is replaced by the beautiful feeling that God is for you and has a unique plan for your life. Know that what happens in someone else's life has absolutely nothing to do with yours.

Back before cell phones were commonplace, it was critical to have a watch when you traveled. There was no other way to tell time except for public clocks. I had a particular watch I liked to wear on the road. It was nice and comfortable. It kept accurate time too. I had just returned from consulting with a church in Sweden when I received a small package from the pastor's associate and his administrator—a beautiful Rolex Presidential watch! Yes, the one with a solid gold face and diamonds all around it. Unfortunately, this one was fake, but boy, did it look real. I'm sure the guys sent it to me as a half gift, half joke.

As I packed for a trip to consult with a Missouri church, I was arranging all my usual items when I realized I couldn't locate my favorite watch. The nice, comfortable one. As the time drew near for me to leave for the airport, I knew I had a decision to make—go watchless or wear the fake Rolex watch. I reluctantly picked the knockoff Rolex. I was nervous I would not know what time it was.

After the plane landed and I was riding in the car toward our meeting place, I did my best to keep the watch as out of sight as I could. It stood out, and I wasn't sure how the pastor might respond to someone in my position wearing it.

Finally, our meeting began—just the pastor and me sitting across a table from each other in a conference room. After a couple of minutes of small talk, I noticed the pastor was wearing a beautiful Rolex himself. I began to feel more comfortable—until he looked at me, then my watch, and asked, "Is that a fake?"

"Yes," I replied.

"Mine is too," he said.

We both laughed and still chuckle about it now, thirty years later. The only difference now is that he has a *genuine* Rolex, and I'm using my cell phone to tell time. When image becomes more important than truth (reality), there is a reason—and a problem. Many people live by the saying "just as I'm not," instead of "just as I am."

Speaking of "just as I am," several years ago famous author and evangelist Billy Graham wrote a book that was essentially his life story. That book was titled *Just As I Am.* This was an excellent title for his book because it was based on the song he played at nearly every crusade.

At the same time that Billy Graham's book was published, another book was released, ironically or coincidentally, with the exact same title, *Just As I Am.* That book was a gay novel.

Now, I know this example could leave you feeling perplexed, but it reflects the fact that titles are not copyrightable. In fact, I went to a local bookstore and saw Billy Graham's book prominently displayed, and wouldn't you know it, only one table over, I saw the exact same title . . . that novel, *Just As I Am.*

Both books appeared the same on the outside with their matching titles, but what a difference on the inside!

Writer Mary DeMuth reflected, "The Christian life is not about managing your reputation so you look like a Christian. It's about handing Jesus your heart, your will, your emotions, your ambitions (everything really), and asking Him to live His amazing life through you. The first is playacting; the other is genuine Jesus-loving faith."

We should be the same person privately, publicly, and personally. Oscar Wilde writes, "Most people are other people. Their thoughts are someone else's opinions, their lives a mimicry, their passions a quotation." My second book's title summed it up well: *You're Born an Original—Don't Die a Copy*. Be inspired, but don't copy. Nothing is more inspiring than a confident person who doesn't pretend to be something or someone they're not.

If you're someone else when you're with others, the next time you're together, you'll have to remember who you were the last time. If you're going to be weird, be confident about it.

Becky Lehman noted, "Self-esteem is typically defined as confidence in one's own worth or abilities. As a Christian, I define self-esteem as having confidence that I am who God says I am. It's not dependent on my own abilities (because those can be so unreliable!), but instead on knowing that God will equip me for the work He has set out for me to do." Your self-esteem will be solid as long as you keep in mind this one timeless truth: God loves you just the way you are—but He loves you too much to leave you the way you are.

Is faking it a way of life for you?

For some people, it's not merely fake it until you make it. It's fake it until you fake it until you fake it until you fake it. Be careful who you pretend to be. You might forget who you are.

One of the greatest compliments anyone can give you is to say, "You're different." Christians live in this world, but we are aliens. We're destined for another place; this earth is not our final destination. We should talk differently, act differently, and perform differently. We should stand out.

There should be something different about you. If you do not stand out in a group, if there is not something unique or different in your life, you should reevaluate yourself. Take a close look at your thoughts, conversations, and actions, and ensure they're your own. Be yourself—who else is better qualified?

I've never liked dressing up, especially under the onus of a theme. Dress like a cowboy for this party, be a celebrity for this gathering, wear clothes from the sixties for this celebration. Some people love this, but I don't. In fact, I have been excited to get an invitation to something only to discover I had to be a farm animal or some other uncomfortable thing. So I just don't go to those events.

I'm not saying that dressing up in some outrageous outfit is wrong—far from it. It's just that when our whole lives are one disingenuous costume, conversation, or action, that's what drives me crazy. Too many people are "dressed up" in something other than themselves and spend their whole lives that way.

Wanting to be me has been in me since I was born into this world back in the midfifties. I like my genuine self, and I prefer others that way too. I think God also does. The Bible says in 1 Corinthians 12:18 that it *pleased* Him how He made us. God made you and me exactly as He wanted, yet there's still room for improvement.

Imagine God with a great big smile on His face the day you were born. And Him smiling even wider every time you're genuinely being *you*. For some reason, that's easy for me to picture.

When I worked at a publishing company, we decided to create a study Bible using the King James Version (the version the disciples used . . . just kidding!). It was to include commentary from all our prominent authors.

In collecting samples to study, I came across a Bible with the words *Genuine Imitation Leather* stamped in gold foil on its back cover. I immediately thought that was a funny saying, maybe like the expression "jumbo shrimp," which also makes me laugh.

Sometimes this kind of "leather" is called pleather. It looks like the real thing, but it's fake and plastic. Whether that bothers you is based on your opinion of leather. And that's my point: we should all value what God values—our genuine selves.

As I looked at the *Genuine Imitation Leather* imprint, I thought, *Many of us Christians are like this. Genuine but living an imitation life. Sincere but not ourselves. Dedicated but not free. Doing the best we can but full of regrets.* Like this Bible packaging, we want to appear to be respectable and valuable, but we're an imitation of what we think people want us to be.

How do we get here? We don't start out that way. If there's genuine *anything* in the world, it's a baby. We begin life completely real and honest. From infancy through the start of school, we're generally thinking, *Why not?* Anything is possible.

Kids are genuine because they always ask questions and are open to viewing the world from many viewpoints: the sports hero, the superhero, the prince or princess, the clown, the mommy or daddy, and others. They create stories and imagine different ways to use ordinary things, like making drums out of household items or a hat from nearly anything.

What they feel from the inside, they do. This is what my grandchildren do every day.

I believe there's something inside of every person crying out to be who God created them to be. Not a job title, a status level, or a physical achievement—but that person they know they genuinely are.

15 | Thoroughly Enjoy Minding Your Own Business

There's one action guaranteed to cloud your mind and get you off track—meddling in other people's business. The more you get involved, the more you'll be sucked in. Like a sponge, other people's troubles absorb your best ideas and energies. Don't intrude into matters that don't concern you. It only creates more problems.

Proverbs 20:3 says, "It is an honor for a person to cease from strife, but every fool quarrels" (NET). Instead, turn away from trouble and toward your destiny. Successful people never worry about what others are doing. Worry about your own sins; you will not be asked about someone else's. How will getting involved in other people's issues and problems help you pay your bills?

Alaska was one state I'd never been to until I received an invitation to speak at a conference hosted by a thriving church in Anchorage. It was a two-day conference, and I was honored to be the guest speaker. The conference was going very well, with overflow crowds on both sides of the church's aisle.

I was well into my message on the first evening when right in the middle of my talk, a man shouted out, "Does that apply to your wife too?" Slightly stunned at the interruption, I replied, "Of course." I continued speaking, all the while wondering what that was about. To this day, I don't remember what I said that prompted his question.

As I was ending my message, I noticed all the ushers positioning themselves along the walls near the front of the church. As I closed the service and walked off the platform, I saw the man who had shouted out during the service walking briskly toward me. Simultaneously, all the ushers began to converge in my direction to position themselves between this man and me. I began to wonder if this guy was dangerous.

Before the man could get to me, I was entirely encircled by the ushers. Still, he was able to call out to me, "I'm sorry for saying that while you were speaking."

I told him, "No problem," and he left without further incident.

After the service, I went to dinner with the pastor and his wife. I couldn't help but ask, "What was the deal with the guy who spoke out tonight?"

The pastor looked at me with a "you won't believe this" expression. He said, "The man you heard in the service has been in our church several years. He is a former police officer. His beat was the airport. A year or so ago, he was working and got into a dispute with a teenager out near the airport.

The altercation escalated, and the youth fled. He pursued the young man, got into a scuffle with him, shot him, and killed him."

Apparently, it was unclear whether the killing was justified, and the police officer was currently under investigation.

He continued, "Furthermore, I learned the whole incident had affected his personality and his family. His wife left him and took off with another man. She was here tonight, with the other man, right across the aisle from him. That was the reason for his comment, 'Does that apply to your wife too?' There was also a shooting a year ago of a minister in a service nearby, so everyone was aware of that."

Everyone except me, I thought.

What did I learn from this? Sometimes less is more. Sometimes it's better not to know everything. And it's always better to stay out of other people's troubles.

Can you imagine my state of mind if I had known all this while I spoke? I'm sure I would have been distracted and not as focused as I should have been. Although I somehow put my words into this man's situation between his wife and him, I certainly didn't do it on purpose. I know better!

They say milk is good for your teeth. Do you know what else is good for your teeth? Minding your own business. To keep all of your teeth, (1) brush, (2) floss, and (3) mind your own business.

> Like one who grabs a stray dog by the ears
> is someone who rushes into a quarrel not their
> own. (Prov. 26:17 NIV)

Don't trouble trouble until trouble troubles you.

Dr. Steve Maraboli asked, "How do I have productive days with minimum drama? Simple; I mind my own business." Nothing will bring you greater peace than staying out of other people's business.

"Stay out of the fray," a wise man once told me. The more you get involved, the more you'll be sucked in. Your best ideas and energies will be absorbed in the turmoil of someone else's troubles. Avoid opinions about things for which you have no responsibility. Change the channel, leave the heated online thread, stop the gossip, and stay in your own Hula-Hoop.

Make yourself happy today by minding your own business. Instead, turn toward your destiny. The best thing you can do is mind your business, grow your business, handle your business, and stay away from messy people who are always in everyone's business.

"Mind your own biscuits and life will be gravy," sings Kacey Musgraves.

16 | Someone Else's Victory Is Not Your Defeat

A bus carrying only ugly people crashes into an oncoming truck, and everyone inside dies. As they stand at the pearly gates waiting to enter paradise and meet their maker, God decides to grant each person one wish because of the grief they have experienced.

They're all lined up, and God asks the first one what their wish is. "I want to be gorgeous," they say, so God snaps His fingers and it is done. The second one in line hears this and says, "I want to be gorgeous too."

Another snap of His fingers, and the wish is granted.

This goes on for a while, with each one asking to be gorgeous, but when God is halfway down the line, the last guy in the line starts laughing. When there are only ten people left, this guy is rolling on the floor, laughing his head off.

Finally, God reaches this last guy and asks him what his wish will be. The guy eventually calms down and says: "Make 'em all ugly again."

You can always find someone prettier than you, more successful than you, with a better family than you, with more opportunity than you, with more money than you; envy is insatiable. A more productive way to think is to compare yourself to yourself, or maybe it's better to compare yourself with what God's plan is for your life. God gives you everything you need to succeed with His plan. Appreciate what you have—this will make you a more positive and productive person since you'll no longer be comparing yourself.

Someone else is happy with less than what you have. Someone else would love to trade places with you. I'm sure billions of people around the world would gladly give up what they have in exchange for what you have. Develop instead an abundance mentality—a grateful attitude for all you have and all you've escaped. Two things define you: your patience when you have nothing and your attitude when you have everything.

Remember these words from Elizabeth O'Connor: "Envy is a symptom of lack of appreciation of our own uniqueness and self-worth. Each of us has something to give that no one else has." Envy is a waste of time. You already have all you need to begin what God wants you to do.

When you allow envy to dominate your life, you can't help but notice that everyone has more than you. Or so you think. Nothing is as it appears. The truth is, envy has a special power, a special kind of magnet that draws you to things that seem so much better than whatever it is you have or don't have.

Job 5:2 says,

> Surely resentment destroys the fool,
> and jealousy kills the simple. (NLT)

Never do the envious, jealous, and insecure stuff. Be the hustler, the well-wisher, and the go-getter. Jealousy looks terrible on us, yet too many of us continue to wear it.

Tony Gaskins said, "Never envy. You don't know what a person had to go through to get what they have. You don't know what they are going through to keep what they have. Focus on your life and keep working to make it better." Envy is a mirage, and what you think you see in someone else is probably not really there.

When something good happens to someone else, it takes nothing away from you. Instead, notice the people who are happy for your happiness and sad for your sadness. They're the ones who deserve unique places in your heart.

Every person is probably tempted to be jealous of someone. So next time you're looking at someone and thinking, *I wish I were that successful/pretty/talented*, remember, someone is thinking that about you.

Don't be deceived into counting other people's blessings instead of your own. Galatians 6:4 says, "Let each one examine his own work. Then he can take pride in himself and not compare himself with someone else" (NET). Proverbs 14:30 reminds us,

> A heart at peace gives life to the body,
> but envy rots the bones. (NIV)

There was a hunter who came into the possession of a special bird dog. The dog was the only one of its kind because it could walk on water. One day the hunter invited a friend to go hunting with him so that he could show off his prized possession.

After some time, they shot a few ducks, which fell into the river. The man ordered his dog to run and fetch the birds. The dog ran on water to fetch the birds. The man was expecting a compliment from his friend about the amazing dog but did not receive it.

Being curious, he asked his friend if he had noticed anything unusual about the dog. The friend replied, "Yes, I did see something unusual about your dog. Your dog can't swim!"

More than 90 percent of the people we face every day are negative. They choose to look at the hole in the middle rather than the doughnut. James 3:14–16 says, "But if you have bitter envy and selfish ambition in your heart, don't boast and deny the truth. Such wisdom does not come down from above but is earthly, unspiritual, demonic. For where there is envy and selfish ambition, there is disorder and every evil practice" (CSB).

So do your best to rid your heart of envy, malice, jealousy, hatred, and unforgiveness. That'll release you to have gracious speech from a pure heart for others. You will never be disappointed with that choice.

17 | Go to Sleep with a Dream and Wake Up with a Purpose

I had the opportunity to work for the largest Christian publisher in America. As vice president and publisher, I oversaw all publishing and book acquisitions from authors in the nondenominational Christian world. In this role, I interacted with many leading ministers and pastors. Of course, quite a few other people wanted to contact me to see if we would publish their books as well.

I'll never forget one such encounter. I received a call from a man I had heard about but didn't know personally. As soon as our conversation began, he told me he had five great book ideas and that they would easily sell a million copies each. (Telling this to a person with my experience is not a great idea.) I listened to what each book was about. They were decent ideas but nothing particularly unique. And there was no way they would sell as many copies as he thought.

I think he could sense my hesitancy because he continued to up the ante with his sales pitch. He said, "I'm blessed, and if you do a book with me, you'll be blessed." I had heard this line before. He continued to tell me that I would make millions because of my association with him.

So I decided to ask him a question. I said, "*Why* are you writing these books?" hoping he would share a good motive behind them.

Instead, he told me, "Well, I want to be rich!" I remember thinking, *I thought you were already wealthy.*

I told him I needed a couple of days and then I would get back to him. I was 99 percent sure I knew what my decision would be. I called him back a couple of days later and told him we had to pass on his books because they weren't the right fit for us at that time. He was angry about my decision. He told me I was "missing God" and urged me to reconsider. I said my answer was final, but I wished him the best.

Only a couple of years later, that man was all over the national news—a major marital fight in public, a messy divorce, and lots of other junk exposed. Hearing this hammered home to me how important purpose is. The *why* behind your actions and ideas matters a great deal.

Jacob Nordby said, "You know how every once in a while you do something and the little voice inside says, 'There. That's it. That's why you're here' . . . and you get a warm glow in your heart because you know it's true? Do more of that."

What makes you come alive? When do you look to God and say, "Lord, please let me do more of that for others"? Your mission should scare you a little and excite you a lot.

If you can't figure out your purpose, figure out your passion. Your passion will lead you right into your purpose. Henry Mencken observed, "You come into the world with nothing, and the purpose of your life is to make something out of nothing."

You can't pour from an empty cup.

> The purpose in a man's heart is like deep water,
> but a man of understanding will draw it out.
> (Prov. 20:5 ESV)

Fill up on your purpose, and you'll be able to share it with others.

How amazing is it that the same God who created mountains, oceans, and galaxies looked at you and thought the world needed one of you too? When you start seeing your worth from God's point of view, you'll find it harder to stay around people who don't.

An unknown author once wrote, "Your life has a purpose. Your story is important. Your dreams count. Your voice matters. You were born to make an impact." Have a vision for the future so you won't be stuck in the past.

I've also heard it said to "be fearless in the pursuit of what sets your soul on fire." In the words of Martin Luther King Jr., your prayer should be, "Use me, God. Show me how to take who I am, who I want to be, and what I can do, and use it for a purpose greater than myself."

If you really want to hear God laugh, tell Him your plans and exactly how *you* are going to achieve them. Instead, invite God in. Ask Him what His purpose is for your life and how He wants you to achieve it. The Lord promises,

> I will instruct you and teach you in the way you
> should go;
> I will guide you with My eye. (Ps. 32:8)

Your greatest wealth is God's presence with you. There is a persistence to direction. The Bible says,

> Many are the plans in a person's heart,
> but it is the LORD's purpose that prevails. (Prov.
> 19:21 NIV)

Ideas go away, but direction stays. There's a persistence to God's direction and purpose.

Be a person with a mission, not just out fishin'. Evangelist R. W. Schambach put it this way: "Be called and sent, not up and went." You are a person with a purpose, not a problem. Purpose fuels passion. Find something to live and die for.

I'd like to ask you an important question: Is God finished with you? It may feel like He's given up on you or He could never use you like you once thought He could. But there's something deep inside you that says, *God has put me together a certain way, on purpose for a purpose.* Sometimes you feel unsettled because you know you are meant to do more. Ironing boards are surfboards that gave up their dreams and got a tedious job. Don't be an ironing board.

Never underestimate the purpose of the gifts within you. They are given to you so you can fulfill to the fullest God's calling in your life and affect the souls who are connected to your gifts. Dolly Parton advised, "Everything God does is purposeful. And since God is in each of us, each of us has a purpose. Figure out who you are, then do it on purpose."

People are waiting to be affected by the purpose God has placed within you. Your most significant contribution may not be something you do but someone you raise. Tony Evans said, "When you realize God's purpose for your life isn't just about you, He will use you in a mighty way." Now go do it!

18 | Miracles Come in Moments

I was invited to speak at an early morning devotional for twenty minutes. I remember working on my notes for the talk on a legal pad with green pages. I don't think I'd ever used green paper to speak from before, nor have I used it since. My notes for this talk included thirty-five points. Little did I know then that covering many ideas in a short amount of time would be the basis for writing my bestselling books.

The night before, I went to bed earlier than usual. When I woke up, I wasn't asking my typical questions. *What time is it? What should I wear? Where did I leave my keys?* No, instead, my very first thought was *An Enemy Called Average.* Yes, I believe God was giving me not only a title for my talk but also an excellent title for the book I was writing.

I wrote that phrase at the top of my notes and then later proclaimed to my audience, "Today, I want to share with you about an enemy called average." After my speech, I had several people come up to me and say, "That's a great book title." I told them with a smile, "I know, it's mine—don't take it!"

I didn't know how much that phrase and that book would impact my life and the lives of hundreds of thousands of others worldwide.

I kept my original notes on that green legal paper. Recently, my daughter, Michelle, surprised me by beautifully framing them. When I opened her gift, it brought tears to my eyes as I remembered how God, in His love for people, gave me that phrase. It was God's miraculous deposit into my heart that morning.

To paraphrase Oral Roberts, let's live expecting a miracle. I don't mean in a strange sense, where we overspiritualize everything, but in a way where we're aware that the maker of the universe is our Father. And He is able to *do anything, anytime, anywhere.* When you choose—yes, choose—that mindset, your perspective will automatically change.

I am a realist: I expect miracles at any time. I try my best to have a holy suspicion that God is up to something good every day. Sometimes God drops something in your lap for you to share and make others better. He does that because He loves people. He trusts you and me to do something with it to bless others.

Miracles happen every day, so never stop believing. The moment you're ready to quit is usually the moment right before a miracle happens. God can change things very quickly in your life. Open your heart and invite God into every circumstance, because when He enters the scene, miracles happen.

The question is not, "Does God speak?" The question is, "Are we listening?"

Stop every day and look at the size of God. Who is God? What is His personality? What are His character traits? According to the Bible, He is everlasting, just, caring, holy, divine, omniscient, omnipotent, omnipresent, and sovereign. He is light, perfection, abundance, salvation, wisdom, and love. He is our Creator, Savior, Deliverer, Redeemer, Provider, Healer, Advocate, and Friend.

> The LORD is the great God,
> the great King above all gods. (Ps. 95:3 NIV)

I often travel by air, and one of the benefits is the glimpse I get of God's perspective. I like looking at my challenges from thirty-seven thousand feet above the earth. I can see that no problem is too large for God's intervention and marvel that no person is too small for God's attention.

God is always able. If you don't need miracles, you don't need God. Dave Bordon, a friend of mine, said it best: "I don't understand the situation, but I understand God." Live boldly. Push yourself. Don't settle.

God likens our life in Him to seedtime and harvest. Do you realize how miraculous that is? Let me give you a conservative example: Suppose one kernel of corn produces one stalk with two ears, each ear having two hundred kernels. From those four hundred kernels come four hundred stalks with one hundred sixty thousand kernels. This huge harvest is a result of one seed planted only one season earlier.

The miraculous realm of God involves multiplication and increase that benefit many. That one phrase God gave me opened the door to speak to millions of people around the world.

Think miraculous thoughts. Look for God working on your behalf. Believe in His Word. Fill your mind with supernatural ideas. Ask your heavenly Father to help you renew your mind and understand how much He loves you. Our confession to the Lord should be Jeremiah 32:17: "Ah, Sovereign LORD, you have made the heavens and the earth by your great power and outstretched arm. Nothing is too hard for you" (NIV).

God is bigger than _____ (fill in the blank for your own life).

Writing my first book started as a dream, an impossible kind of hope. Sometimes I wonder if I ever would have finished that book without that divinely given title.

You and I have two ways to think about our lives. We can live our lives as though nothing is a miracle or everything is a miracle. I choose the latter. How about you?

19 | Keep Going— Everything You Need Will Come to You at the Right Time

decided to be a business administration major at the beginning of my freshman year of college. I concluded that this degree would offer me the best postcollege job opportunities, and I admired my dad, a businessman. I enrolled in the basic freshman-level business courses—principles of management, economics, and accounting 101.

I'll never forget my first day in accounting class. Since I hadn't decided to study business until a few weeks earlier, I quickly discovered that most of my classmates had taken bookkeeping in high school. This gave them a basic understanding of accounting, so I felt like I was already two months behind on that very first day.

Our instructor was a top-rated teacher. He was also known to be demanding and gave tests no one could complete on time. Moreover, I didn't like the subject. It almost felt like a foreign language to me. If you know anything about accounting, most of it flies in the face of logic. Many numbers you think would be debited are posted as credits, and credits are posted as debits. It is confusing, to say the least.

The final kicker was that accounting was required to graduate with my chosen degree. Two years of it! I was determined to give it my best, and candidly, my loftiest goal was to get a C. That was the minimum required. It was tough for me.

Each of our homework assignments was to be completed on green ledger paper with a no. 2 pencil. I remember taking hours to do each task, and there were a lot of them! After spending hours on one assignment, I just couldn't get it to balance. And balancing a ledger is the fundamental goal for all accounting. As much as I tried, I was off by eleven cents!

What happened next made me somewhat of a legend in the business school. I did what made sense to me. I taped a dime and a penny to my homework and gave it to my instructor with this note: "Here is the eleven cents I can't find in this assignment. I hope this takes care of it. I plan to go into marketing and make enough money after I graduate to have someone else do my accounting for me. Sincerely, John Mason."

Here's the point. One of the biggest understatements in the Bible is this:

> "For My thoughts are not your thoughts,
> Nor are your ways My ways," declares the LORD.
> "For as the heavens are higher than the earth,

So are My ways higher than your ways
And My thoughts than your thoughts." (Isa. 55:8–9
NASB)

It's impossible to imagine all that God can do. He may not always give you what you want, how you want it, and where you want it. You can try to treat Him like an on-demand God, but that isn't how He moves in your life. Trust me, He has a better plan.

Humanity says, "Show me, and I'll trust you." God says, "Trust Me, and I'll show you." His solutions are vast. His way is infinitely higher than our ways, and it is perfect. Sometimes He will deliver you directly from your situation, but sometimes He'll find a way around or through it for you.

I'm not saying God directed me to tape that money to my homework (that would be a stretch), but I do know there are many ways God can get you where He wants you to be. Don't limit Him. Be open to every idea and path He provides for you.

Without faith, we cannot please God. Margaret Shepherd observed, "Sometimes your only available transportation is a leap of faith."

God promises to extend wisdom to those who ask in faith. True peace comes from knowing that God is in control. Sometimes the best thing you can do is not think, not wonder, not imagine, not obsess. Just stop and have faith that everything will work out for your good. I have heard it said to always believe in God because there are some questions that even Google can't answer.

If an undertaking doesn't include faith, it isn't worthy of being called God's direction. Persevere—God has something for you that only you can fulfill. Stay the course. God is still writing your story. Don't let go of your faith because of what you have yet to see. Someday you'll know why it was all worth the effort.

People who wonder whether the glass is half empty or half full miss the point. The glass is refillable.

When you live by faith, you're stronger than you imagine, Jesus is closer than you realize, and you're loved more than you know. God has ruled in your favor. Nothing and no one can overturn that ruling. He has determined your situation's outcome and proclaimed blessings, victory, breakthrough, healing, and deliverance over you. He is the final authority. He is predictably and most assuredly working all things together for your good.

God wants each of us to come through whatever situations we face. God has perfect timing for everything. Learn to wait on Him. This brings Him honor and you peace.

We are not to be moved by what we see but by what we do not see. This is what the apostle Paul meant when he wrote that "we walk by faith, not by sight" (2 Cor. 5:7).

Today is the day to begin to walk by faith—right out of your present circumstances.

20 | The Best Thing to Appreciate in Life Is Each Other

Not long after the Affordable Care Act (also known as Obamacare) became law, we received a most unusual call in our office. The caller identified herself as a top leader within the United States Department of Human Services. She said her team was responsible for the implementation of Obamacare and they desperately needed encouragement. If anyone needed a boost, these folks did.

It seems she had read my book *An Enemy Called Average* and was now inviting me to speak to the entire leadership team of about fifty top government staffers. The group included many significant civil servants from several branches of the government. She also let me know that these leaders were not political appointees but long-term employees. Some agreed with Obamacare and some didn't. Nevertheless, it was their job to make it work, as they had for President George Bush's prescription drug program a few years earlier.

At first, my daughter, Michelle, who took the call, thought it was a prank. The rollout of this program had been a huge challenge, with troubles regarding its website, availability, and information—the list went on and on.

I talked at length with the caller about their situation and how they had worked day and night, weekends and holidays, trying to right this enormous government ship. Most workers had taken very few days off since this had become law. These employees were senior executives, with most having worked for the federal government for twenty or thirty years or more.

She also informed me about guidelines for speakers—no religious comments and no political views. That roomful of employees would be as diverse as I could imagine, with people of every religious, political, ethnic, sexual, and philosophical persuasion imaginable.

I was out of my comfort zone. *Right where I'm supposed to be*, I thought. God was stretching me, and I knew that when He does that, I never return to my original shape. I was excited!

I prepared, working on what I was going to say—and what I wasn't. I felt confident I could serve them well with my talk. And they were allowing questions after I finished, something I enjoy doing.

On the day of my talk, security was tight. A senior military leader picked me up, and when we arrived at our destination, I went through several checkpoints. As I sat in the car and journeyed toward the meeting, I had begun to have a thought I couldn't shake. These individuals were faithfully doing their jobs under enormous pressure, and they were being hammered with criticism they had done nothing to deserve. I knew what I had to tell them.

I'm sure you've done this. You see a military person or a police officer dressed in uniform, maybe on a plane, in a store, or at a public event. You go up to them and say, "Thank you for your service." It made you feel good, and hopefully, it made them feel good too. I began to feel this way toward these civil servants, not only for their work amid the uncertainty in this law but also for the decades of service they had given to our country and to me.

After being introduced, I stood before the group. The look in most of their eyes told me they'd rather be somewhere else. *Anywhere else.* It was not a friendly Sunday-morning crowd. I told them I had something to say to them from my heart before I began. I looked out into the crowd, making eye contact with as many people as possible, and said, "Thank you for *your* service!"

You would not believe the immediate change in the countenance of everyone I could see. A simple word of encouragement, a thank-you, was given. It was so powerful.

The talk went well. The questions afterward quickly went from business to personal, and people opened their lives to me. I shared from my life how I depended on God to help me.

As we ate a catered lunch together afterward, many people came up to me and said, "I've been working for the government for twenty-plus years, and no one has ever thanked me for my service. You did. You will never know how much that meant to me."

I had no idea those simple words—*thank you for your service*—would touch people so deeply. Never underestimate the power of a simple thank-you or a random compliment. How long has it been since you've thanked those closest to you or those you interact with every day? Just imagine for a moment what your life would look like if you did.

Never waste an opportunity to tell someone that you love and appreciate them, because you never know, tomorrow could be too late. An excellent way to appreciate someone is to imagine your life without them.

Reach out and appreciate those closest to you every day. Because what you do every day matters!

I believe our genuine self is a grateful self. One that is appreciative of others. A simple thank-you or an encouraging word can be powerful. You don't have to agree on everything; just be there with a "word spoken in due season" (Prov. 15:23). You'll be surprised at the good it might do. When you see something beautiful in someone, tell them. It may take a second to say, but for them, the compliment could last a lifetime.

Open up your day to a life of gratitude and see your whole world change. The atmosphere of your life will be forever impacted. Giving thanks and saying grace isn't just a prayer before a meal; it's the best way to live.

Be thankful for what you have. Your life, no matter how bad you think it is, is someone else's fairy tale. No matter how challenging your life becomes, do more than stay strong; stay grateful. Stop stressing and recognize all your blessings.

Do you count your blessings, or do you think your blessings don't count? A person is wise when they don't long for the things they don't have but are thankful for those things they do have. Do you have an attitude of gratitude? Today?

Cicero observed, "A thankful heart is not only the greatest virtue, but the parent of all other virtues." Being thankful affects every area of your life. Max Lucado writes, "The devil doesn't have to steal anything from you; all he has to do is make you take it for granted."

If you aren't grateful for what you have, how could you be happier with more? Francis Schaeffer said, "The beginning of man's rebellion against God was, and is, the lack of a thankful heart." Saying thanks is not a sign of weakness, it's a sign of strength. What if you lost everything then miraculously gained it all back? How thankful would you be?

If you continually compare what you want with what you have, you'll be unhappy. Instead, compare what you deserve with what you have, and you'll be happy.

No duty is more urgent than that of returning thanks. How long has it been since you thanked those closest to you? Or those who help you every day?

How many of us would like people coming into our lives every day with appreciative and positive words? I know I would. Everyone likes to be appreciated. God's Word says to "be obedient . . . knowing that whatever good anyone does, he will receive the same from the Lord" (Eph. 6:5, 8). What you make happen for others, God will make happen for you. The encouraging words you sow into others have a way of coming back to you.

William Arthur Ward spoke wisely: "There are three enemies of personal peace: regret over yesterday's mistakes, anxiety over tomorrow's problems, and ingratitude for today's blessing."

Replace regret with gratitude. Be grateful for what you have, not regretful for what you don't have. Successful people take what they have, are thankful for it, and then make the most out of it. Appreciation changes everything. Gratitude changes everything!

What would your life (family, relationships, business) look like if you spent the next twenty years being genuinely, deeply grateful? For example, no matter what kind of house you live in, wouldn't you rather be there than in the best hospital in your city?

Did you know that if you have cash in your wallet and a jar on your dresser that collects loose change, you are considered "prosperous" by more than 90 percent of the world's population? If you have food in a refrigerator, clothes in addition to the ones you are wearing, and a roof over your head at night, you are more fortunate than 75 percent of the people in the world.[1] Think about it: at any given moment, a billion people would gladly trade places with you.

A friend of mine recalled a conversation they had with an exchange student from an impoverished nation. As they compared and contrasted her experiences in the United States with those in her home country, she remarked, "You Americans get to complain about the nicest things."

When you feel like complaining, bring God into the situation.

> You will keep him in perfect peace,
> Whose mind is stayed on You. (Isa. 26:3)

If things aren't going well, stop and be thankful for what you do have. Because God starts with what we have to take us from where we are to where He wants us to be.

I never cease to be amazed by God's faithfulness. His love—everlasting; His grace—abounding; His mercy—new every morning; His only Son—given for us!

Here's some powerful advice: start your day with gratitude and end it with thankfulness. Today is thanksgiving day! Count your blessings at every opportunity. Take some time every day to reflect on all you have to be thankful for. Don't find yourself at the end of your life saying, "What a wonderful life I've had! I only wish I'd realized and appreciated it sooner."

Psalm 9:1 instructs,

> I will give thanks to you, LORD, with all my heart;
> I will tell of all your wonderful deeds. (NIV)

What would your life look like if you spent the next twenty years being genuinely, deeply grateful to God and others?

Studies have shown that even the most introverted person will have contact with more than ten thousand people in their lives. Just think of the impact you can have for good by being kind and appreciative everywhere you go.

Kind words do not cost much, yet they accomplish much. They bring out the good in others. Appreciative words are one of the most powerful forces for good. So start some appreciative words on their travels. There is no telling where the good they may do will stop.

21 | Anything That Costs You Your Peace Is Too Costly

I had fallen into today's modern trap. Yes, I found myself in a debate online. I knew full well that no one had ever won an argument on social media, but here I was wasting precious creative writing trying to convince somebody I was right and they were wrong.

I found myself thinking about these conversations during my day, and as I did, I felt the heat of anger inside me. I daydreamed of my responses and found myself giving my best time to the worst use of my creativity. This kind of thinking was not only a waste, but it was also infecting other areas of my life. It had to stop.

At the height of my entrapment, I found myself in a vigorous debate with three different people. My choice to engage in these unproductive conversations was robbing me of my peace. I didn't fault these people; I faulted myself.

I had allowed them into my life, and it cost me. I knew I couldn't make everyone happy—I wasn't coffee! I knew I had to change my mindset with action. Then I discovered the "unfriend" and "unfollow" options.

With the click of a button, these distractions were instantly gone from my life. I moved on in peace. I no longer cared about what these people said or did and quickly realized how much better my life was without seeing or reading their posts. When they were "deleted," I felt immediate peace. My mind quieted. The quieter it became, the more I could hear. Erin Plewes advised, "Listen in the silence. It has quite a story to tell."

To find peace, you have to be willing to lose your connection with the people, places, and things that create all the noise. Take that step. Consider walking away from people and situations that put you down, threaten your peace of mind, lower your self-respect, undermine your values, compromise your morals, and diminish your self-worth. Stop responding to rude, critical, argumentative people, then watch how peaceful your life will become. Anything that costs you your peace is too costly.

I've always said, "I don't get into fights with ugly people because they have nothing to lose." But I learned I have something to lose: my peace. Sometimes you just need to put up a sign that says, "Temporarily closed for spiritual maintenance."

Brilliant things happen in calm, uncluttered minds. Be peaceful and allow yourself to grow stronger. Isaiah 30:15 says, "In quietness and confidence shall be your strength." Silence is a source of great strength. "I've told you all this so that trusting me, you will be unshakable and assured, deeply at peace. In this godless world you will continue to experience difficulties. But take heart! I've conquered the world" (John 16:33 MSG).

Inner peace comes not from getting what we want but from remembering who we are in Christ Jesus. One of the most courageous decisions you'll ever make is to finally disconnect from what causes the chaos and hurt in your life. Move toward where you find peace. Connect with God and accept this promise from Him: "And the peace of God, which surpasses all understanding, will guard your hearts and minds through Christ Jesus" (Phil. 4:7).

22 | The Right Time Is the Right Time

For some reason, out of the blue, I began to have headaches. These were not migraines, but they were very annoying. I was sensitive to noises and music, and the pain would just never go away.

Over time I became concerned about these headaches, so I went to see a neurologist. He cleared me of any significant problems, but he also suggested I talk to a counselor. I'd never been to a counselor before, but these headaches had been going on for months, and they were beginning to get the best of me. So I decided I would talk to a counselor.

I met with a therapist named James (not his real name). I'll never forget our first meeting. I began to tell him exactly what was going on. He asked some questions, and the meeting lasted forty-five minutes.

I remember thinking, *I can't understand what happened. It seems like we just talked, but I feel a little better.* My counselor told me that we should meet again five more times, so we set up the appointments.

Each one of the counseling sessions followed the same format. We would talk for maybe forty-five minutes, and then I would leave. He asked reasonable questions, nothing too invasive or probing, but they seemed to be helping me. At the last session, he told me he thought he had a solution that would work for me. The solution? *To do nothing.*

"Do nothing? What do you mean?"

He said, "I mean, you need to take some time to do nothing. Go away to a quiet, peaceful place and do nothing."

I thought, *I could do that. I think so, anyway . . .*

I came home and told my wife. "Linda, here's what the counselor has suggested, based on all five counseling sessions: that I do nothing."

I made plans to stay in a condo on a small, still lake in Florida. I didn't bring my laptop, golf clubs, or anything else—just my clothes and some money for food.

For a week, all I did was sleep, walk around the pond, and take in an occasional movie. Most importantly, I did *nothing.* I returned from my one week away and I felt better, but I wasn't entirely well. After a few months of occasionally taking time off and doing nothing, my headaches went away.

I was in a season of rest, but I didn't realize it at first. I had been going ninety miles an hour. God had been telling me to slow down, but I hadn't listened. I mean, isn't that what diligent Christians do? I soon realized there was a purpose in my season of resting and waiting.

One of the greatest Bible truths is, for *everything*, there is a season. This thought has helped me gain the proper perspective of where I am today and where others find themselves.

Respect the season of life that others are in. The movie character Madea said, "Some people'll come in your life for a lifetime, and some'll come for a season. You got to know which is which. And you're gonna always mess up when you mix those seasonal people up with lifetime expectations." Watch out for people who always treat everyone the same and don't respect the season other people find themselves in.

Seasons do change. According to Christine Caine, "God prunes us when He is about to take us into a new season of growth and expansion." Don't let someone else tell you what season you're in. If you do, you'll discover the season they say you're in will probably match their need, not necessarily yours. You'll feel out of season, like you're wearing a bathing suit outside in the middle of winter.

It's okay to say no. *No* is a powerful word. Say no to those who don't have your best interests at heart. Say no to those who see in you only what they can get out of you, no matter what season you're in.

Don't be in such a rush to get to another season that you miss what God wants you to learn about yourself here and now. If you pick the blossom, you must do without the fruit.

Every next season in your life will demand a different version of yourself. Only God can turn a caterpillar into a butterfly and sand into pearls. Embrace the season God has for you.

Did you know that the best shortcut you can ever take is to do what God says in His timing? Shortcuts outside the will of God invite compromise and create strife and confusion.

Understand that you're a long-distance runner, not a sprinter. As a marathoner, you don't need to look for shortcuts that open the door to compromise.

Once you know God's will and timing, you should instantly obey, acting without delay. When God is telling you to do something now, delay is disobedience. I have found this to be true: the longer you take to act on whatever God wants you to do, the more unclear His directives become. Make sure you're on God's interstate highway and not in a cul-de-sac.

Ours is a God of velocity. Velocity is all about timing and direction. Since these two always go together, it's never wise to act on only one without the other. Jumping at the first opportunity seldom leads to a happy landing. Solomon writes, "Do not go out in a hurry to argue. Or what will you do in the end, when your neighbor puts you to shame?" (Prov. 25:8 NLV). Even the right direction taken at the wrong time is a bad decision.

So say yes to God, now. Seek His timing and direction. When you find both and act accordingly, you'll find yourself right where you want to be.

23 | How Old Is Your Attitude?

A mother and father had twin boys who were six years old. Worried that the boys had developed extreme personalities—one was a total pessimist, the other a real optimist—their parents took them to a psychiatrist.

First, the psychiatrist treated the pessimist. In an attempt to brighten his outlook, the psychiatrist took him to a room piled to the ceiling with brand-new toys. But rather than yelping with delight, the little boy burst into tears.

"What's the matter?" the psychiatrist asked, baffled. "Don't you want to play with any of the toys?"

"Yes," the little boy said, bawling, "but if I did, I'd only break them."

Next, the psychiatrist treated the optimist. Trying to dampen his outlook, the psychiatrist took him to a room piled to the ceiling with horse manure. But instead of wrinkling his nose in disgust, the optimist emitted a yelp of delight that the psychiatrist had been hoping to hear from his brother, the pessimist. Then the optimist clambered to the top of the pile, dropped to his knees, and began gleefully digging out scoop after scoop with his bare hands.

"What do you think you're doing?" the psychiatrist asked, just as baffled by the optimist as he had been by the pessimist.

"With all this manure," the little boy replied, beaming, "there must be a pony in here somewhere!"[1]

When you can't find the sunshine, be the sunshine no matter how gloomy the forecast. Don't ever let anyone dull your sparkle. I would rather be annoyingly positive and optimistic than destructively negative and hateful. What you allow to consume your mind controls your life.

Whatever we think about, dwell on, and contemplate forms our mindset. Positive or negative. We are what we think, and that is a choice we can make. We cannot control circumstances, but we can control how we feel about them. If we think about excellent things, we'll tend to respond to life excellently. Philippians 4:8 says, "Finally, brothers, whatever is true, whatever is honorable, whatever is just, whatever is pure, whatever is lovely, whatever is commendable, if there is any excellence, if there is anything worthy of praise, think about these things" (ESV). Fill your thoughts with right things, and wrong things will have no place to land. Don't pursue happiness; create it.

So far, you've survived 100 percent of your worst days. One small positive thought in the morning can transform your whole day. Do your best to train your mind to discover the good in every situation.

Don't ruin a good today by thinking about a bad yesterday. Today is the day you prayed for. Miracles are coming to you or past you every day. A beautiful day begins with a beautiful mindset. The happiness of your life is directly connected to the quality of your thoughts. A positive mindset separates the best from the rest. Positivity wins.

Let it go. Don't let the world make you hard. Being negative only makes a difficult journey more difficult. You may be given a cactus, but you don't have to sit on it. If you're not lighting any candles, don't complain about being in the dark. If you keep telling the same sad story, you will keep living the same sad, small life. Jon Kabat-Zinn observed, "You can't stop the waves, but you can learn how to surf."

Not every day will be good, but there is something good in every day. Watch your attitude. It's the first thing people notice about you. A baby mosquito came back after his first time flying. His dad asked him, "How do you feel?" He replied, "It was wonderful! Everyone was clapping for me!" Now, that's a positive attitude.

You and I are responsible for the results in our lives. If we want different results, we need to change our thoughts and actions. So choose hope—now anything is possible. Positive thoughts should advance to positive actions, which lead to positive results.

Audrey Hepburn noted, "Nothing is impossible. The word itself says, 'I'm possible.'" Impossible is just an opinion. The apostle Mark writes, "Jesus said to him, 'If you can believe, all things *are* possible to him who believes'" (9:23). And Matthew 19:26 declares, "Jesus looked at them and said, 'With man this is impossible, but with God all things are possible'" (NIV). Impossible is where God starts.

You can choose to live in the front row or the last row. Zig Ziglar observed, "Positive thinking will let you do everything better than negative thinking will." Lead a takeover in your life. Throw out the tyrant of negativity and replace it with a life of hope.

When the odds are one in a million, be that one. The question isn't who will let you, it's who's going to stop you. Nobody regretted thinking his best and giving his best. Beautiful things happen when you distance yourself from negativity and embrace a positive mindset.

24 | Nothing Is as It Appears—Nothing

O n nine occasions, I've had the privilege to speak at the excellent Increase Conference in Hawaii that Bob Harrison of Harrison International hosts. I know what you're thinking—suffering for Jesus, right? These events are held at beautiful resorts right on the ocean in Kauai and Maui or on the Big Island. I have a very good time, and my wife, Linda, always comes along, which makes it even better.

One time we stayed on the Big Island at a hotel that was exceptionally beautiful and popular to tourists from not only the United States but also Japan. The décor reflected popular art, statues, and structures from both cultures. There were many tasteful Buddha statues, along with a lot of American landscaping and furnishings.

One sweltering day I was sitting outside at the pool. Being a somewhat rotund person, with only a few hairs left on top of my head, I found myself sitting cross-legged, shirt off, in a shaded area. After only a few minutes, I noticed a group of six couples looking at me, pointing their fingers my way, and talking among themselves. A minute or two later, they all began to walk solemnly toward me. As these couples arrived in front of me, each one slowly bowed down and started to act like they were worshiping me.

Okay, I'm kidding. This didn't happen.

Every time I'm in Hawaii and this "Buddha-body boy" tells this story, the crowd pauses, then lets out a big laugh. So I couldn't resist sharing it with you to make a point. What you see isn't always what you get. As I've always said, "A good picture is one that doesn't really look like you." Hall of Fame coach Lou Holtz hit the nail on the head when he said, "Nothing is as good as it seems and nothing is as bad as it seems. Somewhere in between there, reality falls." Nothing is as it seems, but God is everything He's made out to be.

Life is full of opposites, and so is the Bible. In fact, I believe one of the primary reasons the Bible was written was to teach us to expect the opposite. Faith in place of fear. Peace instead of confusion. Health in place of sickness. God's light instead of darkness. Furthermore, we're instructed to be humble, then we'll be exalted; show mercy, then watch mercy come to us; give, and it will be given to us; be weak to become strong; serve to become a leader; and be last to be first. Opposites.

Calvin Coolidge advised, "We do not need more intellectual power; we need more moral power. . . . We do not need more of the things that are seen; we need more of the things that are unseen." According to the apostle Paul, "What is seen is temporary, but what is unseen is eternal" (2 Cor. 4:18 NIV). And let's follow Smith Wigglesworth's example: "I am not moved by what I see. I am not moved by what I feel. I am moved by what I believe!"

What is unseen is more real than what is seen. Look beyond what you see and be on the lookout to "see the unseen" in your life. The invisible God and the Holy Spirit are at work in your life.

25 | Better Things Are Coming

'm a former high school basketball coach. I know people who meet me in person don't automatically think, *He coached basketball.*

Despite being vertically challenged at five-foot-eight, I loved coaching basketball. And for a long time, I thought I would even make a career out of it. I felt very natural doing it. Because the private Christian school where I coached was not a member of the state athletic association, we could do pretty much what we wanted.

For four years, I was an assistant coach, and we had a typical schedule where we played only other Christian schools. But when I became the head coach, I signed our team up for seven different tournaments and scheduled games against as many public schools as possible. We played a forty-two-game schedule—and won 75 percent of those matchups!

I had kids from all around town wanting to play for me, and I found myself in their homes talking to their moms and dads about coming to the school. It was crazy. My arrangement with the school was only as a coach. I didn't teach. For me, that was perfect.

My assistant coach was also the athletic director. He had never coached basketball before, but he did the best he could. I was doing all I could to develop a stellar basketball program and grow as a coach.

After my second successful season, I set up an entire summer league schedule for our team, started an off-season conditioning program, and persuaded a former NBA player to be a volunteer coach. I attended a top-flight coaches' clinic and was looking forward to another great season.

A couple of days before school began, I received a call from the school's superintendent requesting a meeting. As I walked into his office, I could tell something was up. He had a strange look in his eyes. With a trembling voice, he said I would not be coaching basketball that upcoming season. He said my assistant coach had come to him and stated that *God had told him he was supposed to be the head coach.*

I was hurt, angry, and confused. My assistant had never coached before. I understood better than anyone how little he knew. I also knew that every assistant coach in America "hears a voice" telling them they can and should be the head coach. That doesn't make it God's voice, and it certainly doesn't make it true.

I told the superintendent this was a mistake. His only response was, "God said that to him, and we didn't know that you wanted to come back." Really? I'd been their head coach for two years and had just finished coaching the team that summer. There was no question the program was successful and moving in the right direction. I said I was going to talk with the pastor (his boss) about this. I left the office, stunned.

The meeting with the pastor began by him thanking me for coaching, and then he repeated the assistant coach's "God told him he was to be the head coach" line. I said, "Every assistant coach in America hears that voice!" But he wasn't listening to any of it.

I finally told him, "I feel like leaving this church, but I'm not going to." (I believe in running *to* something, not *from* something.) Leaving offended is never what I want to do.

The pastor said, "If we did make a mistake, we will admit it to you, and we'll bring you back." I said okay and left, but I knew in my heart it was over.

The season started in November. By December, they were already interviewing new coaches. By February, they had hired another coach who was also a full-time teacher. I never heard a word from anyone.

I'm sure there was no ill intent from anyone at the school, the pastor, or my assistant coach. My relationship with them continued to be good for several years afterward.

What is most important to know is this: when things happen beyond *your* control, it doesn't mean *God* is not in control.

The bottom line is this: people will do what they want to do. They will hear what they want to hear and see what they want to see. At the end of the day, God is in control, even when a person tries to get in the way.

I never coached at a high school again. But God was still working on my behalf, even if others were not. The Lord connected me later that year with the father of one of the boys I coached. That relationship took me directly to the publishing world, where I would learn to help authors. I also uncovered my desire to write books. Because I had coached basketball, I found my highest calling outside of basketball. Proverbs 19:21 says,

> You can make many plans,
> but the LORD's purpose will prevail. (NLT)

God often puts us on (or takes us off) a path to bring us somewhere completely different from where we expect. Remember, He is in control, no matter what people do. He will get you to where He wants you to be "in due season" (15:23) if you won't give up.

His plans will always be greater and more beautiful than yours. Sometimes you're not given what you want because something better is planned for you. God closes doors because it's time to *move* forward. He knows you probably won't move unless your circumstances force you to. Trust the transition.

Here's what I do: Accept what is. Let go of what was. And have trust in God with what will be. Tomorrow could be the day you've prayed for. Life gives you another chance every day.

Here are amazing promises from God:

> The steadfast love of the LORD never ceases;
>   his mercies never come to an end;
> they are new every morning;
>   great is your faithfulness. (Lam. 3:22–23 ESV)

Every single day you live, our heavenly Father gives you new, everlasting mercies. I don't know about you, but I need this! Thank Him every day for His mercy.

Later, I did have the privilege of coaching my youngest son David's basketball teams as he grew up. He went on to play Division I college basketball! He later became a high school basketball coach and now owns the largest basketball training business in Oklahoma. He's worked with more than thirty NBA players and numerous college basketball players.

It's been said, "Where you are today is no accident. God is using the situation you are in right now to shape you and prepare you for the place He wants to bring you into tomorrow. Trust Him with His plan even if you don't understand it."

So pray this: "Dear God, if today I lose my hope, please remind me that Your plans are better than my loftiest dream." Martin Luther King Jr. said, "We must accept finite disappointment, but we must never lose infinite hope."

You may not always understand why God allows things to happen, but you can be confident He's not making any mistakes. God's way is way better than your own. His plan is bigger than your plans. His dream for your life is more rewarding, more fulfilling, and better than you have ever dreamed of. Now, stay open and let God do it His way.

26 | Question Everything

love to ask questions. I'll admit, it drives my wife crazy sometimes—question after question after question. I've even written two books about questions, *Ask* and *Why Ask Why*.

Have you found yourself in a situation where you didn't feel the freedom to ask a question? An environment where the very act of asking made people think that you doubted or you weren't "on the team"?

Gary Hopkins suggested, "Questions are only offensive to those who have something to hide." However, the right question can change the direction of your life. I'm glad I knew the right question to ask.

When I was a senior in high school, I was offered a four-year, full-tuition scholarship to attend a prestigious college in Indiana. It was an honor to be offered such an excellent opportunity.

At the same time, I applied to a different school that was a Christian university in another state. I visited this school on a college weekend, where I remember feeling a closeness to God that I had never felt before. It was a new university and on the rise. It was a long way from home, but I was excited about the possibility. The bad news was that they offered me zero scholarships, and I hadn't even been accepted.

The college in Indiana invited me to their college weekend, which included a day or two in the dorm/fraternity, extensive campus tours, and a persuasive presentation about why they were the best school in the state. They were recruiting me like an athlete. It was a beautiful campus with first-class academics. And it was *free*. Over the weekend, I noticed they had beer machines in the hallways and girls everywhere in the dorms, and rumor had it . . . strippers were coming in.

I remember walking alone on that campus thinking, *Should I go here or not?* As I pondered my future choice, a question came to me that would eventually change my life.

I asked myself, *What kind of person am I going to be four years from now if I go here instead of the Christian university?* The moment I asked that question, the answer became apparent.

I want to affirm that God calls people to secular schools, but in my case, I knew, *based on my question*, where I should go. I chose the Christian university. The answer to that question was a defining moment in my life. I met my wife, established lifelong friends, and learned about God in a way I never would have had I chosen the other school.

Questions are powerful. Unfortunately, many leaders and organizations discourage them. Never let yourself become attached to or a part of something that discourages or doesn't allow questions. It's a bad sign if you can't ask questions. Questions bring growth.

Is the truth afraid of questions? No, the truth welcomes questions. They bring answers and freedom.

If you go to an elementary school, you will find a class full of questioners. The kids might ask, "Why is the sky blue? Why do we have ten fingers and toes? Why can't birds talk, but I hear them singing? Why don't I have eyes in the back of my head like I hear people say?" They ask insightful, probing questions. If you talk to most middle-aged people, you won't find that! They've become incurious. They've lost something from their childhood.

A well-known Chinese proverb says, "He who asks a question is a fool for five minutes; he who does not ask a question remains a fool forever." Tim Ferriss advised, "The way you become world-class is . . . by asking good questions."

God asked Moses, "What is that in your hand?" (Exod. 4:2). Two things we all have in our hands are (1) our story and (2) our gift. God wants to use both for His glory.

Ask yourself these questions:

If everyone in the United States of America were on my level of spirituality, would there be a revival in the land?

Does the devil know who I am?

Has failure gone to my head?

Am I running from something or to something?

Who do I need to forgive?

What one impossible thing am I believing and planning for?

Is there anything I can't let go of that I know I should?

What is my most prevailing thought?

Am I doing what I truly want to do?

What good thing have I committed to do that I have quit doing?

Am I known for the promises I don't keep?

How old is my attitude?

What outside influences are causing me to be better? Worse?

Does my reach exceed my grasp?

Am I becoming ordinary?

When was the last time I did something for the first time?

What is one thing I can do for someone else who has no opportunity to repay me?

You are where you are today because of the questions you've asked—the questions you've asked yourself and the questions you've asked other people. To go where you want to be, you have to ask the right questions. Life's most important answers are found in asking the right questions.

27 | Have Fun (Seriously)!

Quite a few years ago, I was presented with an interesting opportunity to be a substitute teacher for several weeks. I was looking forward to it. I had decided ahead of time I would follow the specific curriculum they asked of me, but I would present it in a much more interesting, entertaining, and fun way. I was hopeful the students and I would enjoy the experience.

I thought things were going well until I had an encounter with the assistant principal. I was walking down the hall when I heard a voice from behind me say, "Mr. Mason, I need to talk to you—now." She came right up beside me, looked me straight in the eye, and said, "We have a problem. The kids are having too much fun in your class, and we don't have fun here at this school."

I wanted to ask her, "Is what you believe so fragile, so ineffective, that you can't enjoy life with a smile?" But I didn't. What I knew, that she obviously didn't, was that it's okay to enjoy life. It's okay to have fun, smile, laugh, and have a good time.

A grim countenance does not equal a more spiritual experience. I try to follow this philosophy of life; I want to hire a person who whistles while they work. I like to sing at the office, even though it's mostly a joyful "noise."

My wife, Linda, and I laugh every day. Even in the most challenging situations, we have found ourselves laughing. I remember right after I had heart surgery (yes, the kind where they open your chest), I had to ask her to leave my hospital room several times because being around each other was causing us to laugh—and every single laugh was causing a great deal of pain right in the middle of my chest. We have the kind of relationship where we can sit around doing nothing but still have fun because we're together. A smile is an inexpensive way to improve our looks—and I need all the help I can get!

The old saying is true: if you can laugh at it, you can live with it. You know your life needs to change when someone asks you what you do for fun, and you can't even remember the last time you had fun. Life is to be enjoyed, not endured. Dale Carnegie reflected, "People rarely succeed unless they have fun in what they are doing."

Having fun isn't unspiritual. You don't always need a logical or biblical reason for doing everything in your life. When you're having fun, you're making memories. Life on this earth comes around only once. So why not do what makes you happy and be around people who make you smile?

Christians should be the happiest, most enthusiastic people on earth. The word *enthusiasm* comes from the Greek word *entheous*, which means "God within" or "full of God." "Happy are the people whose God is the LORD" (Ps. 144:15).

Smiling—proof that you are happy and enthusiastic—is a choice. Enthusiasm and joy and happiness will improve your personality and people's opinion of you. It will help you keep a proper perspective on life. Helen Keller said, "Keep your face to the sunshine, and you cannot see the shadow."

The bigger the challenge you're facing, the more enthusiasm you need. Philippians 2:5 says, "Have the same mindset as Christ Jesus" (NIV). I believe that Jesus was a man who had a smile on His face and a spring in His step.

Your attitude always tells others what you expect in return.

A smile is a powerful weapon. It can break the ice in challenging situations. You will find that being enthusiastic is like having a head cold; both are very contagious. A laugh a day will keep negative people away.

Many people say, "Well, no wonder those people are happy, confident, and positive; if I had their job and assets, I would be happy too!" Such thinking falsely assumes that successful people are positive because they have a good income and possessions. But the reverse can be true. Such people probably have a good income and lots of possessions due to being positive, confident, and happy.

Joy always inspires action. No significant accomplishment has ever been achieved without enthusiasm. In John 15:10–11, the Lord promises, "If you keep my commands, you will remain in my love, just as I have kept my Father's commands and remain in his love. I have told you this so that my joy may be in you and that your joy may be complete" (NIV).

Your life doesn't get better by chance. It gets better by choice. Choose fun. Pick laughter. Smile more; it adds to your "face value." And do what Mark Twain said: "Forgive quickly. Kiss slowly. Love truly. Laugh uncontrollably."

28 | Denying the Truth Doesn't Change the Facts

More people would learn from their problems if they weren't so busy denying them. This mindset has become a doctrine of denial. Instead, face the facts, take action, and watch God show up on your behalf.

I made a phone call to a friend I knew wasn't doing very well. I started our conversation by asking him, "How are you doing, Leon?"

He began to talk in a preprogrammed kind of way, saying, "Everything is super good! I'm blessed beyond measure! Things are fantastic!"

I let him finish.

Then I asked him, "Leon, how are you *really* doing?"

He quietly said, "Not so good."

"How can I help?" I responded. Now we were making progress.

Denying a problem doesn't make it go away. It usually only makes it worse. How can you fix something if you don't know or admit what's wrong?

Unfortunately, in many Christian environments, you're not allowed—or supposed to have—problems. Sometimes leaders are the worst in this regard. The problem with this theology is that now the only things they can talk about are their successes. They can't talk about their difficulties because admitting they have them would uncover the reality that they don't always walk in victory.

As a result, you tend to hear leaders talk only about their high points, which creates a distorted image—a unique breed of supermen and superwomen with supernatural powers. They're never discouraged, they're never troubled, they never have anything wrong with them. They become legends . . . inaccurate ones.

What are you going to do with your problems if you're not supposed to have any? How are you going to solve your problems if you're not allowed to admit you have them?

What you can't say owns you. What you hide controls you.

The freest person in the world is the one who has nothing to hide. Don't be fooled. People aren't always what they "post" themselves to be on social media. Dr. Steve Maraboli observed, "You can speak with spiritual eloquence, pray in public, and maintain a holy appearance . . . but it is your behavior that will reveal your true character."

Denying the facts does not make them go away. Saying something is super good when in truth it's super bad is simply not telling the truth. Denying the bone is sticking out does not heal the compound fracture in your arm. The "doctrine of denial" is empty, and walking by *fake*, not faith, never works. These kinds of ideas can lead to dishonesty, deception, fraud, and lying.

Denying a problem never helps solve it. The truth always comes out in the end, no matter how hard anyone tries to hide it or stop it. Denial is just a temporary delay of the inevitable, which, in the worst cases, is an angry disappointment with God based on inaccurate belief.

The truth is the truth, even if no one says it. A lie is a lie, even if everyone believes it. You should always be able to tell your husband or wife exactly how you feel about everything. And be honest with God; besides, He already knows what you're thinking.

Sometimes you can tell more about a person by what they hide than by what they show. Not saying something or hiding something on purpose is just the same as lying. You and I are to walk by *faith*, not by *fake*. Honesty is always the best policy. How can we help others without it?

How can we confess our faults to one another if everyone says they don't have any problems? How can we grow if we don't overcome obstacles that we say we don't have? Be honest. God already knows the facts and is ready to work them all together for your good.

29 | You Can Hear for Yourself

Today, I give you permission to ignore some people. To erase their words and actions against you and your mind. To delete their ulterior motives and replace them with God's plan for *your* life, not theirs. Sometimes you need to act like some people never crossed your path.

People will eventually show their true colors. So when someone shows you who they truly are, don't try to paint a different picture.

Saying "no" and "no longer" can deliver you from thoughts of defeat, confusion, and wasted time. The truth is that God has a beautiful plan for your life, and nothing can stop it except you. Not everyone has a right to speak into your life.

Once upon a time, a beautiful, independent, self-assured princess happened upon a frog in a pond. The frog said to the princess, "I was once a handsome prince until an evil witch put a spell on me. One kiss from you, and I will turn back into a prince. And then we can marry, move into the castle with my mom, and you can prepare my meals, clean my clothes, bear my children, and forever feel happy doing so."

Later that night, while the princess dined on frog legs, she kept laughing and saying, "I don't think so."

I've spent a lot of my adult life as an executive in the publishing world and as an author. I guess that's like being a director and an actor. Seeing both sides of publishing is enlightening and frustrating.

I spent some time as the head of a publishing company in Florida. I felt God had led me there from Tulsa to help turn the company around. It had floundered for years, and the owner was seriously considering closing it down. Miraculously, God used our team to quickly make the business very profitable.

After nearly three years there, I started to feel my assignment was nearing an end, so I began to consider other publishing possibilities. One such opportunity that presented itself was starting a new company with two people I had worked for in publishing before, along with a longtime friend of mine. This time, I was going to be the president and a 25 percent owner.

My previous employment with these two men had gone well, except for one issue. While I worked for them, I wrote and self-published my first book. They distributed it, and it became one of their top two bestselling books the first year. You might think everyone would be happy about that, but that was not the case, as I would find out.

One year after the book's release and with sales of more than one hundred thousand copies, I was called into a meeting with the general manager, my boss. He said he needed to talk with me about my book. The meeting began with a summary of my sales and a bizarre comment. He looked at me and said, "The owner wants you to know that if he had known how well your book would sell, he would not have wanted you to write and publish it." I was stunned and confused at the statement.

He continued, "He feels it's a conflict of interest for you to be an employee here and also an author."

My only response was, "What about all the people who my book has helped? Hundreds of thousands!"

He did not answer.

I also knew the publishing house had made a significant profit by distributing my book, with no risk to itself. This all happened at a time when it was in desperate financial need. The publishing house had even asked to borrow money from me that year to pay an urgent bill from a company that was threatening to force them into involuntary bankruptcy!

I thought this was a very strange conclusion, and I saw no negatives for anyone because my book had sold so well. Yet the owner and my boss believed what they told me. Why would I now start a new publishing company with them if they still had a problem with me being an author? It was a good question, so I met with that owner I'd worked for previously to ask him. He looked me in the eye and told me it would not be an issue since now I'd be an owner, like him. With that matter addressed, we started the company. I left Florida and moved back to Tulsa, now a part-owner and president.

Things were moving along well at our new venture. Good authors were showing interest and signing up to do books with us. Then I got a call from my longtime friend and partner. He said he needed to come by my house to meet with me *that* night. He warned me that the next day the two other owners were going to demand I resign and give back all my stock. To say I was shocked was an understatement! The company was only three months old!

I walked into the meeting that next day not knowing what to say or think. Immediately, the man whom I had worked for previously looked at me and said, "We need you to resign; God *told me* you're not supposed to be involved in publishing. We feel it's a conflict for you to be an author and involved in publishing."

Incredulous, I responded, "God hasn't told *me* that!" I knew this man was either lying to my face now or had lied to my face three months before when we started the company. Either way, he was showing his true self.

I wasn't buying it. I certainly wasn't falling for his line that "God told him." God doesn't speak through people with ulterior motives. And He certainly talks to a person directly first.

But my business partner wasn't budging and neither was the other partner, and all the while, my longtime friend was caught in the middle. I felt I had been played. I had been lied to. I had risked a lot and now was being forced out.

I thought, *How can you lie to a person's face and then use God's name to "seal the deal"?* That was dangerous and something I would never consider doing to someone else. (Later, my longtime friend told me he had heard him use that same "God told me" line many times on numerous other people.)

Fortunately, my wife, Linda, could see things clearly, and she lovingly talked with me about the right path forward. I'll never forget what she said: "They've shown you their true colors. You shouldn't be in partnership with people like that. We've been delivered! We should celebrate!"

I walked away. It wasn't easy. In the short run, I saw the company start to prosper without me. I felt alone, but I never, ever doubted I did the right thing. I knew I worked for my heavenly Father, and I believed He wanted the best for His child.

If you find yourself in the wrong story, close the book and leave.

Knowing when to walk away is wisdom. Being able to is courage. Walking away with your head held high is dignity.

Here's the rest of the story. A few years later, that publishing company was forced to be sold by the bank holding its note, and its parent company filed for bankruptcy. The publishing company had been close to going under at least two other times. All the stockholders (I would have been one of them) barely escaped losing millions of dollars individually because they'd had to personally guarantee loans to keep the company going.

Here's a good lesson: take notice of those who don't celebrate your victories, and certainly don't partner with them.

Put God first. Know He will take care of you regardless of humankind's devices.

Finally, not everyone will want you to succeed. Some people are jealous, dishonest, or greedy. Most importantly, never fall for the line "God told me" from someone who has ulterior motives. If our loving heavenly Father intends to communicate with you, I guarantee He will (possibly many times) try to speak His will to you first.

Maybe someone has shown you their true colors. It's time to say no to that relationship. Don't let your loyalty become slavery. According to Avinash Wandre, "If they don't appreciate what you bring to the table . . . then let them eat alone."

Some people come into your life as blessings, and others come into your life as lessons. I am thankful this man showed me his true colors. He showed me exactly who I don't want to be. Joyce Meyer writes, "If we are ever going to develop an ability to hear from God and be led by His Spirit, we have to start making our own decisions and trust the wisdom God has deposited in our hearts." We all need to erase the voices that replay in our heads from others who don't want us to be successful.

I know.this is a personal story, and I've been candid. I tell it to help you. If you find yourself relating to my experience, I pray any ill-intended words spoken to you will no longer hold you back. Be free from them. Do what you know in your heart to do. This is your life, your story, your book. No longer let anyone else write it, and don't apologize for the edits you make.

Beardsley Jones challenged, "You have this one life! How do you wanna spend it? Apologizing? Regretting? Questioning? Hating yourself? Dieting? Running after people who don't see you? Be brave. Believe in yourself. Do what feels good. Take risks. You have this one life. Make yourself proud."

30 | Jesus Didn't Say, "Follow Christians"— He Said, "Follow Me"

Do you remember back in the 1990s when people wore those rubber WWJD bracelets? They were a not-so-subtle way to declare a person's faith. Athletes, celebrities, and everyday people of all ages were wearing them.

Charles Spurgeon, a well-known evangelical preacher in London, used the phrase "What would Jesus do?" several times in a sermon on June 28, 1891. He's generally credited with this thought. Charles Sheldon reiterated it in his 1896 book *In His Steps* that was subtitled *What Would Jesus Do?*

The expression was so popular it became a *snowclone*, "a verbal formula that is adapted for reuse by changing only a few words so that the allusion to the original phrase remains clear."[1] People began to say, "What Would Reagan Do?" and "What Would Johnny Cash Do?" Pacifists said, "Who Would

Jesus Bomb?" and atheists said, "What Would Darwin Do?" Advertisers said, "What Would Jesus Buy?"

I even joined in.

Over the years, I got to know a well-meaning but somewhat controlling Christian leader. For comfort's sake, let's call him Jonathan Lee. I used to say I would create a bracelet saying WWJLD, "What Would Jonathan Lee Do?" *Every time*, and I mean dozens of times, I shared my WWJLD idea with any of his followers, they would immediately laugh, nod their head, and with a certain knowing look on their face, admit they thought about him the same way.

Yes, we are to be imitators of God. Yes, we can learn from others' victories and mistakes, insights and experiences. Indeed, God uses others to help us and guide us. But don't fall for formulas from people who may not have your best interests in mind and say, "I did it this way, and you should too!" or "Be like me, and you can have what I have!" Malarkey.

I like this expression: "Be careful when you blindly follow the masses. Sometimes the *M* is silent."

Have you found yourself pondering, *I wonder what Pastor So-and-So would think about this, or what Sister _____ would do?* instead of considering, *What does the Bible say? What has God shown me?*

One of my favorite sayings is from J. G. Stipe: "Faith is like a toothbrush. Everybody should have one and use it regularly, but it isn't smart to use someone else's." Decide for yourself. Learn for yourself. Answer for yourself. Steve Jobs advised, "Your time is limited, so don't waste it by living someone else's life."

There is God's will *in* our lives and God's will *for* our lives. God's will in our lives is the same for everyone. He wants every one of us to know Him, worship Him, walk in His forgiveness, and make it to heaven (and much more!). God's will *for* our lives is different for *every single person.* God may want you to go to Nigeria and start an orphanage; someone else may not feel compelled to help with that cause but feel led instead to volunteer at the downtown rescue mission, teach children in their local church, or be the best Kentucky Fried Chicken manager in history.

I believe when we open ourselves up to WWJLD instead of "What Would Jesus Do," we allow others to become our idols. Not everything you hear from others is what God is saying.

Many times I have prayed for people whose primary source of difficulty was what other people had said to them or about them. I listened to the negative words they said about themselves, and I simply asked, "Who told you that?" Almost every time, they answered with the name of a friend, parent, family member, or coworker. Interestingly, they didn't really believe the words but spoke what others said was true about them.

One of the most powerful questions you can ask of anything you believe is, "Who said it?" Because when you do, you'll uncover whether you should believe it.

You can study, follow, and imitate others but never really know them. They may differ in a hundred ways from what you publicly see and from who you think they are. The Bible says, "Don't copy the behavior and customs of this world, but be a new and different person with a fresh newness in all you do and think. Then you will learn from your own experience how his ways will really satisfy you" (Rom. 12:2 TLB).

Here is the challenge for all of us: that we do not depend too much on others for our personal direction. If we do, we will feel like we've lost our way, but really, we've only let someone else borrow it.

Reclaim your brain. Think and know for yourself. Follow Jesus.

31 | No Excuses

Mr. Jones came into the office an hour late for the third time in one week and found the boss waiting for him. "What's the story this time, Jones?" he asked sarcastically. "Let's hear a good excuse for a change."

Jones sighed. "Everything went wrong this morning, boss. The wife decided to drive me to the station. She got ready in five minutes, but then the drawbridge got stuck. Rather than let you down, I swam across the river as fast as I could, and look, my suit is still damp. I ran out to the airport, got a ride on Mr. Thompson's helicopter, landed on top of Radio City Music Hall, and was carried here piggyback by one of the Rockettes."

"You'll have to do better than that, Jones," said the boss, obviously disappointed. "I don't know any woman who can get ready in five minutes."

Nobody cares about your excuses. But, oh, how they can influence your life.

Quitting, giving up, failing, and even judging—all these begin with an excuse. Never allow an obstacle in your life to become a reason for doing nothing. "You, therefore, have no excuse, you who pass judgment on someone else, for at whatever point you judge another, you are condemning yourself, because you who pass judgment do the same things" (Rom. 2:1 NIV). We Christians should be people who make progress, not excuses. Wake up every morning and throw away all your excuses.

Excuses take you away from reality and are almost always untrue. Instead of dealing with the solution, your mind is focused on how you can escape reality. Excuses dull your mind and fill it with uncertainty. Justification is the language of wannabes. Forget excuses. Learn to admit when you mess up.

If you sow, you will reap. Conversely, if you don't plant because you make excuses, you won't reap. Today's excuses are tomorrow's regrets dressed in disguise.

Empty explanations put distance between you and your dream. Excuses put the brakes on your goals. They add unnecessary time to the pursuit of your dreams and can cause you to miss God's timing. Excuses will always be there, but opportunity won't. Excuses are for people who don't want it badly enough. Always wake up with a smile, knowing today you will have fun accomplishing what others are too afraid to do.

Don't make excuses for why you can't get something done. Focus on all the reasons you must make it happen. There are no excuses, just choices. When you lose all your excuses, you will find the results you dream of. You can have results or excuses . . . not both.

Determination beats justification every time. The explanation of *why* you didn't doesn't produce anything except delay, denial, and disappointment. It's like the adult version of "the dog ate my homework" excuse you tried to use as a kid. Rid your mind of this unproductive thinking.

What is your favorite excuse? How can you replace it with a choice and an action? You can have one hundred reasons why not, when all you really need is one reason why. Stop defending why you didn't do what you know you should have done. Be stronger than your excuses. Tomorrow is a mystical land where 99 percent of all human productivity, motivation, and achievement is stored.

There have always been people who have made up excuses to the Lord. Some knew their justifications weren't true, while others actually believed their own reasons.

Jesus told a parable of the great end-time banquet and the men who were invited to the Lord's table: "But they all alike began to make excuses. The first said, 'I have just bought a field, and I must go and see it. Please excuse me.' Another said, 'I have just bought five yoke of oxen, and I'm on my way to try them out. Please excuse me.' Still another said, 'I just got married, so I can't come'" (Luke 14:18–20 NIV).

These men made excuses and missed out on salvation. All of them made the mistake of believing their reasons rather than believing in God.

Moses and Gideon made excuses to the Lord, yet they recognized their excuses were invalid. When the Lord sent Moses to Pharaoh, Moses said:

"Pardon your servant, Lord. I have never been eloquent, neither in the past nor since you have spoken to your servant.

I am slow of speech and tongue." The LORD said to him, "Who gave human beings their mouths? Who makes them deaf or mute? Who gives them sight or makes them blind? Is it not I, the LORD? Now go; I will help you speak and will teach you what to say." (Exod. 4:10–12 NIV)

When the Lord asked Gideon to save Israel from invaders, Gideon argued, "'My lord . . . how can I save Israel? My clan is the weakest in Manasseh, and I am the least in my family.' The LORD answered, 'I will be with you, and you will strike down all the Midianites'" (Judg. 6:15–16 NIV).

Do not hide behind an excuse. Jesus said, "If I had not come and spoken to them, they would not be guilty of sin; but now they have no excuse for their sin" (John 15:22 NIV). An excuse will keep you from completing the assignment God has for you. Don't let it.

32 | Forgive Your Enemies—Nothing Will Annoy Them More

Once upon a time, two friends were walking through the desert. They argued at some point in the journey, and one friend slapped the other across the face. The one who got hit was hurt and, without saying anything, wrote in the sand, "Today, my best friend slapped me in the face."

They kept on walking until they found an oasis, where they decided to go for a swim. The one who had been slapped got stuck in the mire and started drowning, but his friend saved him. After he recovered from the near drowning, he wrote on a stone, "Today, my best friend saved my life."

The friend who had slapped and saved his best friend asked him, "After I hurt you, you wrote in the sand, and now, you wrote on a stone. Why?"

The other friend replied, "When someone hurts us, we should write it down in sand where winds of forgiveness can erase it away. But when someone does something good for us, we must engrave it in stone where no wind can ever erase it."

Learn to write your hurts in the sand and carve your blessings in stone.

Who do you need to forgive? This is one of the most powerful and healing questions you can ask yourself. You may think this is a spiritual question, but it's also a compelling success, relationship, and mindset question.

If you want to travel far, travel light. Unpack your thoughts of envy, jealousy, unforgiveness, and revenge.

Many people are stuck because they've been offended. Jesus warned us this would happen in the last days. He proclaimed, "And then many will be offended, will betray one another, and will hate one another" (Matt. 24:10). Was there ever a time in history when so many people were mad at other people (most whom they'd never met)? Offense is here to stay until Jesus comes, and we all must learn the power of forgiveness now more than ever.

Unforgiveness does a great deal more damage in the vessel in which it's stored than the object on which it's poured. Without forgiveness, life is governed by an endless cycle of resentment and retaliation. What a waste! Don't say, "Well, you don't know what that person did to me." Just know what unforgiveness will do to you. The only people you ought to try to get even with are those who have helped you. Here's what I've found: successful people have a way of not letting things stick to them.

One Sunday morning before a church service began, people

were sitting in their pews and talking about their lives, their families, etc. Suddenly the devil appeared at the front of the church. Everyone started screaming and running for the front entrance, trampling each other in a frantic effort to get away from him.

Soon everyone was evacuated from the church, except for one elderly gentleman who sat calmly in his pew, unmoving, seemingly oblivious to the fact that God's ultimate enemy was in his presence.

This confused Satan a bit, so he walked up to the man and said, "Don't you know who I am?"

The man replied, "Yep, sure do."

Satan asked, "Aren't you afraid of me?"

"Nope, sure ain't," said the man.

Satan was a little perturbed at this and queried, "Why aren't you afraid of me?"

The man calmly replied, "Been married to your sister for over forty years."

Don't let stuff stick to you. Never underestimate the power of forgiveness to loosen and free you to run after your goals. You can't get ahead while you're trying to get even. What matters is what happens in you, not to you. Forgiveness is essential for good human relationships. You can't give a hug with your arms folded.

Your forgiveness of others assures you of God's forgiveness. Jesus said, "If you forgive other people when they sin against you, your heavenly Father will also forgive you. But if you do not forgive others their sins, your Father will not forgive your sins" (Matt. 6:14–15 NIV). The weight of unforgiveness immensely drags you down. It's a tremendous load to carry in the race you're called to run.

Unforgiveness leads to bitterness, which is a harmful misuse of energy. Pondering a negative situation and plotting how to get even diverts a significant amount of brainpower away from productive thinking. If you keep burning bridges, you'll become isolated and alone, and you'll deal with strangers and enemies the rest of your life. Build bridges; do not burn them.

Vengeance is a poor traveling companion. Every Christian is called to a life of reconciliation (see 2 Cor. 5:18). Trying to get even wastes time and results in unhappiness.

Working with churches throughout America, I have found unforgiveness in every stagnate situation. And conversely, I have found that growing churches talk about future progress, not past problems.

Never underestimate the power of forgiveness to free you to fulfill your calling. Forgiveness is the one power you have over a person who slanders or criticizes you. The further you walk in forgiveness, the greater the distance you put between yourself and the negative situation in your mind.

Forgiveness gives you a spring in your spiritual walk and a second wind in the race of life. To forgive is to set the prisoner free and discover the prisoner was you.

33 | What Comes Out of Your Mouth Goes into Your Life

I recently saw a sign under a mounted largemouth bass. It read: "If I had kept my mouth shut, I wouldn't be here." How true! Don't jump into trouble mouth first. What we say is important. The book of Job reminds us, "How forcible are right words" (6:25 KJV). Speak the truth even though your voice shakes.

Let me pose this question for you: Starting today, what would happen if you changed what you said about your biggest problem and your most significant opportunity?

It's funny how one text, one song, one truth, one mistake, one lie, one word, and one person can change your mood in one second. I don't know if you've had this conversation or not, but last month I turned to my wife, Linda, while we were sitting together in our family room and said, "Just so you know, I never want to live in a vegetative state dependent

on some machine. If that ever happens, just pull the plug."
She immediately got up, walked over, and unplugged the TV.

Our words create our worlds. Someone once said, "Words
are free. It's how you use them that may cost you."

Your words have the power to start fires or quench passion.

Don't be like the man who joined a monastery in which
the monks were allowed to speak only two words every seven
years. After the first seven years had passed, the new monk
met with the abbot, who asked him, "Well, what are your
two words?"

"Food's bad," replied the man, who then went back to
his silence.

Seven years later, the clergyman asked, "What are your
two words now?"

"Bed's hard," the man responded.

Seven years later—twenty-one years after his initial entry
into the monastery—the man met with the abbot for the third
and final time. "And what are your two words this time?" the
abbot asked.

"I quit."

"Well, I'm not surprised," the cleric answered disgustedly.
"All you've done since you got here is complain!"

What you're claiming has a way of reaching back and claiming you.

Proverbs is true:

> Life and death are in the power of the tongue,
>   and those who love it will eat its fruit. (18:21 HCSB)

So don't underestimate the power of your words. The devil
doesn't. Use the right words, and they can move mountains,

but wrong words can bring death and destruction. What is said is not powerless or meaningless. Control your tongue and determine to speak what the Word of God says about your life, opportunities, and obstacles.

One of my favorite Scriptures to pray every day comes from Psalm 19:14:

> May the words of my mouth and the meditation of
> my heart
> Be acceptable in Your sight,
> LORD, my rock and my Redeemer. (NASB)

The words you speak become the world you live in. So think before you speak, because the words you say can only be forgiven, not forgotten.

> Even a fool is counted wise when he holds his peace;
> When he shuts his lips, he is considered perceptive.
> (Prov. 17:28)

Never speak from a place of hate, jealousy, anger, or insecurity. One minute of patience when you're angry will save you days of regret. Evaluate your words before you let them leave your lips. Sometimes it's best to be quiet.

Tony A. Gaskins Jr. said, "Take care with the words you speak, it's best to keep them sweet . . . you never know when you might have to eat them." There's a lot of truth to what our parents taught us: if you don't have anything nice to say, don't say anything at all. After all, wisdom can be shown by what you don't say as much as by what you do say. "In your anger, do not sin. . . . do not give the devil a foothold. . . . Do not let any unwholesome talk come out of your mouths, but only what is helpful for building others up" (Eph. 4:26–27, 29 NIV).

What you say influences others, for good or bad. The words you speak last longer than you think. I've experienced this firsthand, many times. Nearly every month someone will say to me, "John, you said _____ or you encouraged me to _____ or you wrote _____ and it impacted my life." Because of words, I've seen suicides stopped, marriages restored, businesses prospered, and lives given to the Lord. So think before you speak. Never miss an opportunity to give a "word spoken in due season," as Proverbs 15:23 (KJV) says, to another person. Your short comment might make a lasting impression. Proverbs 12:14 promises, "Wise words bring many benefits" (NLT). Speak life-producing words to yourself and others.

I've heard it said that "before you assume, learn the facts. Before you judge, understand why. Before you hurt someone, feel. Before you speak, think."

Proverbs 21:23 advises,

> Watch your tongue and keep your mouth shut,
> and you will stay out of trouble. (NLT)

Frequently, what we say to ourselves in the middle of turmoil adds to the problem instead of offering a solution to solve it. Stop speaking badly about yourself over and over again. Repetition is persuasive. If someone talked to you the way you speak to yourself, you would have kicked them out of your life a long time ago. Instead, talk to Jesus about your troubles. He loves to hear from you.

"Leading behavioral researchers have told us that as much as 77 percent of everything we think is negative, counterproductive, and works against us. At the same time, medical researchers have said that as much as 75 percent of all illnesses are self-induced," noted Shad Helmstetter.

The way you speak to yourself matters. The famous painter Vincent van Gogh said, "If you hear a voice within you say, 'You cannot paint,' then by all means paint and that voice will be silenced." Never say anything to yourself that you do not want to come true. Be careful how you talk to yourself because you are listening. Instead, talk to yourself like you would to someone you love. The most influential person you will talk to all day is yourself.

34 | Stop Yourself from Stopping Yourself

One Sunday morning the pastor noticed little Ronny standing in the church's foyer staring up at a large plaque. It was covered with names and had small American flags mounted on either side of it.

The six-year-old had been staring at the plaque for some time, so the pastor walked up, stood beside the little boy, and quietly said, "Good morning, Ronny."

"Good morning, Pastor," he replied, still focused on the plaque. "Pastor, what is this?"

The pastor replied, "Well, son, it's a memorial to all the young men and women who died in the service."

Soberly, they just stood together, staring at the large plaque.

Finally, little Ronny's voice, barely audible and trembling with fear, asked, "Which service, the 8:00 or the 10:30?"

Amazingly, like little Ronny, it is easy to instantly create worry that never previously existed based on an untruth and wrong thinking. What represents your greatest threat? A competitor, your past, a physical restriction, a family member, or something else? The easiest way to answer that question is to grab a mirror and turn it toward yourself. You see, it's too easy to dismiss your loftiest dreams without even taking the first step.

We're all self-made men and women—we made the mess we're in, and many times we did it all by ourselves. Don't create your own storm and then complain about the mud. Seth Godin said, "Just imagine how much you'd get done if you stopped actively sabotaging your own work."

Life is too short to waste it warring with yourself. Every day God thinks of you. Every hour God looks after you. Every minute God cares for you. Because every second He loves you.

The key is to accept happiness without self-sabotage. Don't be the architect of your destruction. Sometimes you feel like saying, "I saw the devil today, and he looked a lot like me." You are your problem and your solution. According to Dr. Steve Maraboli, "The most liberating and empowering day of my life was the day I freed myself from my own self-destructive nonsense."

When you don't believe in yourself, some way or another, you sabotage yourself. Don't tell yourself you can't; instead, ask, "What if I can?" Jenna Galbut observed, "I find it extremely liberating to see that I was the cause of all my problems. With this realization I have also learned that I am my own solution. This is the great big gift of personal accountability. When we stop blaming external forces and own up to our responsibility, we become the ultimate creators of our destiny." Refuse to give up on yourself and your God.

Don't sabotage yourself when something good happens to you because you don't feel deserving. The truth is what Jesus said in John 10:10: "I have come that they may have life, and that they may have it more abundantly." The Bible also says, "Beloved, I pray that you may prosper in all things and be in health, just as your soul prospers" (3 John 2).

What lies do you believe about yourself? What lies do you keep telling yourself? Where in your life are you poisoning yourself? Be careful what you agree with.

"Be careful how you think; your life is shaped by your thoughts" (Prov. 4:2 GNT). Decide today that there's something you're going to do or stop doing. An old adage says, "Why do you stay in prison when the door is so wide open?"

Stop worrying whether other people like you. Do you like yourself?

"I am—two of the most powerful words. For what you put after them shapes your reality," reflected Bevan Lee. You hear and remember what you say to yourself.

In reality, it's not so much you against the world; it's mostly you against yourself. With God by your side and His Word in your heart, you can beat self-defeat!

Notes

Chapter 2 Fake Diamonds Appear Perfect, but Real Diamonds Have Flaws

1. "Perfectionism," *Psychology Today*, accessed September 3, 2021, https://www.psychologytoday.com/us/basics/perfectionism.

Chapter 3 If God Is Making You Wait, Be Prepared for Great Things

1. Morgan Shoaff, "10 Words Stuck with Mr. Sonnier for 15 Years. They Turned Him from Janitor to Principal," Upworthy, September 9, 2015, https://www.upworthy.com/10-words-stuck-with-mr-sonnier-for-15-years-they-turned-him-from-janitor-to-principal.

2. Shoaff, "10 Words."

Chapter 5 Dear Stress, Let's Break Up

1. "Any Anxiety Disorder," National Institute of Mental Health, accessed September 7, 2021, https://www.nimh.nih.gov/health/statistics/any-anxiety-disorder.

Chapter 20 The Best Thing to Appreciate in Life Is Each Other

1. Canadian Red Cross, *We Are the Lucky Ones*, accessed September 9, 2021, https://www.redcross.ca/crc/documents/What-We-Do/Emergencies-and-Disasters-WRLD/education-resources/lucky_ones_povdisease.pdf.

Chapter 23 How Old Is Your Attitude?

1. Adapted from Tatiana Morales, "Writing for Ronald Reagan," CBS News, July 30, 2003, https://www.cbsnews.com/news/writing-for-ronald-reagan/.

Chapter 30 Jesus Didn't Say, "Follow Christians"—He Said, "Follow Me"

1. Dictionary.com, s.v. "snowclone," accessed September 13, 2021, https://www.dictionary.com/browse/snowclone.

John Mason is an international bestselling author, minister, executive, author, coach, publisher, and noted speaker. He's the founder and president of Insight International and Insight Publishing Group. Both organizations are dedicated to helping people reach their dreams and fulfill their God-given destinies.

He has authored thirty books, including *An Enemy Called Average*, *You're Born an Original—Don't Die a Copy*, *Let Go of Whatever Makes You Stop*, *Proverbs Prayers*, *Believe You Can*, and *Know Your Limits—Then Ignore Them*, which have sold over two million copies and are translated into forty different languages throughout the world. His books are widely regarded as a source of godly wisdom, scriptural motivation, and practical principles. His writings have been published in *Reader's Digest* and numerous other national and international publications. In addition, seven of his books have reached number one on an Amazon bestseller list.

He's been the president of two Christian publishing companies. He's also a former vice president and publisher for Thomas Nelson, the sixth-largest book publisher in the world and largest Christian publisher.

As an internationally recognized executive author, coach, and publisher, he's helped numerous prominent authors with their books for more than thirty years. In addition, politicians; players from the NBA, NFL, PGA, and MLB; an Olympic gold medalist; other professional athletes; billionaires; businesspeople; pastors; ministers; New York Times bestselling authors; a Fortune 500 CEO; a Navy SEAL; a top-gun pilot; and a Texas governor have all benefited from his knowledge.

Known for his quick wit, powerful thoughts, and insightful ideas, he is a popular speaker across the US and around the world.

John and his wife, Linda, and their four children reside in Tulsa, Oklahoma.

Author Contact

John Mason welcomes the opportunity to speak at churches, conferences, and various business settings. For more information, to schedule John Mason to speak, or for author coaching and publishing services, please contact:

John Mason
Insight International Inc.
contact@freshword.com
www.freshword.com
(918) 493-1718

If you have any prayer needs, please don't hesitate to contact us. It is a privilege to pray for you.

Find More Wisdom from
John Mason

freshword.com |

Encouragement for Being Exactly Who You Need to Be